D0064880

THE
ADMISSION
OF THE
31ST STATE
BY THE
31ST CONGRESS

An annotated bibliography of

CONGRESSIONAL SPEECHES

upon the

ADMISSION of CALIFORNIA

by

ROBERT G. COWAN

●

LOS ANGELES

1962

PRINTED IN THE UNITED STATES OF AMERICA BY TORREZ PRESS - LOS ANGELES, CALIF.

FOREWORD

The war was not over, although the United States and Mexico were at peace, these United States were not at peace with each other. The Mexican war and its results did not initiate the sectional differences between the various States, but the results were certainly a contributing factor in augmenting many of those differences between the Northern and the Southern States, that culminated in our own civil war.

President Polk was an ambitious Chief Executive, whether it was entirely a patriotic ambition for his Country, or a personal ambition to leave a great name for himself, only he could have had that answer. The cry of "fifty-four forty or fight." advancing our claim for the entire Oregon territory against Great Britain, was resounding about the Nation when he took office. It was quite possible that the wily Polk doubted the outcome of a war with Britain, so the matter was compromised, and the United States came into possession of about one-half of its original claim. After the settlement some complaints could have come to his ear that the Northern States were not entirely satisfied, because the loss of part of Oregon to Britain had thwarted the possibility of a free state or two in this part of the territory; and that the Southern States felt disgruntled by the fact that nothing was acquired for their expansion; and that it would be much healthier for his political future to divert the attention of the Nation elsewhere. Hilliard said, in his speech of February 14, 1850, that it is a fact that the bill for raising men and supplies for the war with Mexico was originally intended to prepare the Country for a contest with Great Britain, over the Oregon question.

Attention was centered on Mexico, and on some vague and flmsy pretexts, the Mexican war commenced. But from the speeches of some comtemporary Congressmen, and not denied, the war was declared only for territorial gain. The Southern States were whole-heartedly in favor of the war, and sent more volunteeers into it than did the Northern States. They visualized additional future slave States out of the acquired territory, to keep the equilibrium between the slave and free States of the Union, or Confederacy, as it was just as often referred to then. There were a few of the thinking statesmen, both from the North and the South, who saw difficulties, increased agitation, and ill will, between the North and South over the additional territory. They were not wrong.

Since the thirteen colonies of Great Britain had made themselves into an independent nation, the balance of the number of free States and slave States had been rigidly maintained. At the time of the Mexican war there were fifteen free States and fifteen slave States. The Southern States had dominated the political scene most of the time since the birth of the Nation. Out of the twelve Presidents, the South had provided all but the two Adams and Van Buren, and was quite jealous of maintaining this position. In the House of Representatives it was in the minority, due to the rapid increase of population in the North, but the balance in the Senate could nullify, or compromise any legislation originating in the House.

According to Meade, of Virginia, most Southern statesmen, when the Federal Constitution was framed, looked to the ultimate abolition of slavery, and strove against that clause which permitted the extended importation of slaves from Africa, from 1788 to 1808. The North insisted upon the clause because the slave trade was so very lucrative. In this interval, with importation and natural increase, the slave population was nearly two and one-half times greater than in 1788. Morehead, of Kentucky, said that in his State, twenty years ago (ca. 1829) there was a strong feeling in favor of some system of gradual emancipation of the slave, but the growing a g i t a t i o n of abolition in the neighbors to the north, and their activities in enticing and decoying away slaves, had reversed the feeling of emancipation. This was also quite true in Virginia and Maryland.

After 1808, the attitude began to change toward slavery in the North. It was not considered so much a moral wrong as it was a detriment to free labor. The cheap labor of Europe could be offset by tariffs, but there had been no way found to compete with the slave labor within the United States. The organization of abolition societies, and their aggressive constant agitation, did much to fix slavery as a permanent institution in the minds of Southern men.

It might be said, that no Congress has convened with more names of great statesmen on its roster than the thirtieth and thirty-first Congress. The names of Webster, Calhoun, Clay, Benton, Seward, Douglas, Cass, Jefferson Davis, Houston, and the then unknown Lincoln are well remembered, but these cast their shadows over many very able men, who would have been outstanding in another Congress. Their ideas, their understanding, their handling of the English language, and, no doubt, their delivery lacks comparison since. But they also had their human side; the show, on occasion, of irritability, of temper, of even some violence, and name calling. "Doughface" was a popular name for an unpopular politician, at the time, defined as a contemptous nick-name for a timid, yielding politician.

Senator Benton, of Missouri, and Senator Foote, of Mississippi, were verbally at each other's throat, and had for some time been using every opportunity in their speeches on the floor of the Senate to indulge in slurring personal remarks. On the seventeenth day of April, 1850, during a speech by Foote, Benton lost control of himself, and in a fit of exasperation, pushed his chair violently from him and strode toward Foote. Foote preceived the move, changed his position to the front of the secretary's desk at the end of the aisle, drew a pistol, cocked it, pointed it to the floor, and waited. He waited until Benton was stopped, and found to have been unarmed, then readily gave up his pistol. In the arguments that followed, Foote challenged Benton to a duel, but it was not taken up by Benton, nor pressed by Foote, who was much the younger man. The investigation of this episode occupies 135 pages in the Government documents.

The treaty of peace with Mexico was concluded February 2, 1848, and the United States, by conquest and purchase acquired what is now California, Nevada, Utah, Arizona, a corner of Wyoming, and parts of New Mexico and Colorado, west of what was not already claimed by Texas. During the two and one-half years to follow, there were numerous attempts in Congress to establish various territorial governments for this region. The slavery question reared its ugly head and all attempts failed. Compromises were tried to appease both the Northern States and the Southern States, but nothing concrete was accomplished until August of 1850.

Throughout most of 1848, Congress was absorbed in debate and speeches on various bills to give Oregon a territorial government, but the subject of a government for California cropped up persistently, always tied up with Oregon. Bills for Oregon were proposed from time to time with amendments added for California, or a government for California was part of the bill. The first of these bills, or compromises, worthy of note, was an elaborate affair of more than thirty sections referred to by some as the Clayton compromise. Primarily it proposed a territorial government for Oregon, but it included a government for Upper California, and another, practically the same as California's for New Mexico, which probably, but at least finally, defeated it in the House, July 28, 1848. The plan was to give California a temporary government, headed by a governor and a secretary to be nominated by the Senate and appointed by the President, for a four year term, or relieved by the President at his discretion. The Federal Government was not to be inhibited from dividing the Territory into two or more, and there was to be no law enacted prohibiting slavery.

Having disposed of the Oregon matter the new Congress went diligently to work for the settlement of a government for California, evidenced by the crop of speeches produced in February of 1849.

On December 11, 1848, Senator Douglas proposed a bill, that was named for him, to make all of the acquired territory into one huge state. It was to be called California and admitted immediately, but to be split into smaller states in the future, as necessity demanded.

On December 20, Smith, of Indiana, reported a bill in the House from the Committee on the territories, to establish a territorial government for Upper California, invoking the ordinance of 1787, which forbids slavery where it is applied.

On January 3, 1849, a resolution of the House was defeated, which was to divide California in two and extend the northern part east to include the white settlement at Salt Lake.

January 16, Douglas read a substitute bill, bounding California on the north by 41° 30' (near the northern boundary of Humboldt county) to 34° 30' (just north of Santa Barbara) on the south, and from the Sierra Nevada mountains to the ocean.

On January 22, Hilliard introduced a bill in the House, authorizing the people of California to form a constitution and a State government.

February 19, Schenck proposed in the House, to cede all of the territory acquired from Mexico, back to Mexico, excepting the land about the navigable waters of the San Francisco Bay and its branches, for which Mexico was to keep the three million dollars already paid her on account. The bill was defeated by a vote of 194 to 11.

February 26, during the course of Evans' speech in the House, he offered a temporary measure for governing California, which practically made the President of the United States a virtual dictator over all of the territory.

Taylor took office as President, relieving Polk, on the fourth of March, 1848. The Executive policy towards California was unchanged, and Congress not being able to agree upon anything with reference to a government for California, went into what has been referred to as a cooling off period.

These proceedings, with an occasional flare-up might have gone on for a number of years without being settled, but the attention of the entire civilized world was drawn to California. Just nine days before the treaty of peace with Mexico was signed, the discovery of gold had occurred, on January 24, 1848, and its attendant influx of population, which reached tremendous proportions in 1849.

The procrastination of Congress had provided no government for California, and left her entirely to herself, except in the matter of customs revenue collections. The de facto government set up by the military was entirely inadequate to meet the needs of the fast growing population. If she was to remain as a part of the United States, it was inevitable that she take matters into her own hands and establish a state government. This was an unprecedented move. No section of the country had heretofore gained admission as a state without some years of territorial existence, and governmental sanction and tutelage. Texas might claim exception to this, but she had a full fledged independent government before she was asked to become part of the Union.

California drew men from all walks of life. The lure of the gold diggings was strong, but not all of the immigrants came with pick and shovel, many had other purposes in mind. Gwin, one of the State's first Senators, left the East with the promise that he would return as Senator. Broderick made the same promise, and both returned East as Senators. Before the close of 1848 the need of a state government was recognized, and by the end of 1849 a convention with a fair representation of Spanish Californians, and Americans from both the Northern and Southern States, had met and a constitution had been drawn. Although this convention is referred to as "The Legislature of a Thousand Drinks," it had done its work well. In framing the constitution, it took what it considered the best from the constitutions of several States, more particularly Iowa, which Gwin favored.

News of the State's action got to Washington, and the President's message, printed under the date of January 24, 1850, informed Congress that the people of California had formed a plan of state constitution, and would soon apply for admission as a State. He recommended that if their proposed constitution is found to be in compliance with the requisitions of the Constitution of the United States, they should be received. He also recommended leaving the people in the balance of the territory the privilege of governing themselves. This opened wide the lid of Pandora's box, and trouble permeated the entire Capitol, and reflected itself throughout the Nation.

The Thirty-first Congress went to work. Bills, resolutions, amendments to bills, and substitute bills were offered. About one hundred seventy speeches were made, which were supposed to have been limited to one hour each, but many speakers were not stopped on the hour. Debates ensued, running into weeks at a time, and many of the remarks made during these debates might be considered speeches. Secession was threatened; this was not the first time, however, that the threat was heard in the Halls of Congress, even Massachusetts had made it a few years earlier. The Congress had the task of deciding upon the admission of California, determining the boundaries of Texas, providing a government for all of the remaining territory, and above all, trying to satisfy the aims of both the North and the South. With the inflammable cloud of the slavery question hovering in the background, but more often in the foreground, the task took on tremendous proportions. It took possession of Congress for the next seven months, to the exclusion of almost all other business.

The Congressmen at Washington found no flaw in the constitution of California, nor any particular fault with it. It embraced, by the unanimous vote of its framers, a clause prohibiting slavery within the State. This, of course, was not entirely agreeable to the Southerners in Congress, but was not the real stumbling-block that caused the protracted delay in voting California into the Union.

Southern statesmen, strong in their constitutional interpretation of State's rights and self determination, knew that eventually California must be admitted as a free State, but they had no slave State to offer to hold the North — South balance in the Senate, so as it was not possible to delay action, as in the past, compromises or concessions must be attached to the California bill. If California was admitted with the boundaries as proposed by the State convention, then slavery would be shut out forever from the Pacific coast, so there was a persistent effort of Southern statesmen to divide the State.

On January 29th of 1850, Clay came forth with his compromise resolutions. Resolved that California be admitted as a State: 2nd, That territorial governments be established for the residue of that which we had acquired from Mexico, without any inhibition

on slavery: 3rd, A settlement of the Texas-New Mexico boundaries: 4th, That Texas be paid for her territorial claims: 5th, To
abolish slavery in the District of Columbia: 6th, To prohibit the
slave-trade in the District of Columbia: 7th, That a more efficient
fugitive slave law be enacted: 8th, Resolved that Congress has
no power to prohibit the slave-trade between slave-holding
States. After a couple of months of speeches and debates the
matter was referred to a committee of thirteen, of which Clay
was the chairman.

On May the 8th, the famous "Omnibus Bill" came out of the
committee in three parts. It was named thus because it carried
so many things, including the gist of Clay's compromise. The
first part involved the admission of California, the Texas boundary settlement, and territorial governments for New Mexico and
Utah. All were eventually voted upon as separate bills, but not
until Congress had wrestled with them for four more months.

On August 13, the Senate voted on the bill to admit California
as a State into the Union. It passed by a vote of 34 to 18. In the
House the same bill was passed by a vote of 150 to 56 on
September 7. The bill was signed by President Fillmore on
September 9, 1850, and California became the 31st State.

SPEAKERS

Alston, William J. Apr. 18, 1850.
Ashmun, George. Mar. 27, 1850.
Atkinson, Archibald. Mar. 1, 1849.
Averett, Thomas H. Mar. 27, 1850.

Badger, George E. Mar. 18, Aug. 2, 1850.
Baldwin, Roger S. Mar. 27, 1850.
Bay, William V. N. Feb. 20, 1850.
Bayly, Thomas H. July 17, 1850.
Bedinger, Henry. Feb. 16, 1849.
Bell, John. July 3, 5, 1850.
Bennett, Henry. May 27, 1850.
Benton, Thomas H. Apr. 8, 22, June 10, 1850.
Berrien, John M. Feb. 11, June 20, Aug. 12, 1850.
Bingham, Kinsley S. June 4, 1850.
Bissell, William H. Feb. 21, 1850.
Bocock, Thomas S. Feb. 26, 1849, June 3, 1850.
Booth, Walter. June 4, 1850.
Bowie, Richard I. June 6, 1850.
Breck, Daniel. Mar. 25, 1850.
Bridges, Samuel A. Feb. 17, 1849.
Brown, Albert G. Feb. 10, 1849, Jan. 30, 1850.
Buckner, Aylett. Feb. 17, 1849.
Butler, Arthur P. Feb. 15, July 9, 1850.
Butler, Chester. June 8, 1850.
Butler, Thomas B. Mar. 12, 1850.

Cabell, E. Carrington. Mar. 5, 1850.
Caldwell, George A. June 7, 1850.
Calhoun, John C. Mar. 4, 1850.
Campbell, Lewis D. Feb. 19, 1850.
Casey, Joseph. Mar. 18, 1850.
Cass, Lewis. Jan. 21, Feb. 12, Mar. 13, June 11, Aug. 12, 1850.

Chandler, Joseph R. Mar. 28, 1850.
Chapman, John G. Feb. 24, 1849.
Chase, Salmon P. Mar. 26, 1850.
Clarke, Charles E. May 13, 1850.
Clay, Henry. Feb. 5, May 13, 21, July 22, 1850.
Clemens, Jeremiah. May 16, 1850.
Cleveland, Chauncey F., Apr. 19, 1850.
Clingman, Thomas L. Jan. 22, 1850.
Cobb, Williamson R. W. June 3, 1850.
Colcock, William F. June 3, 1850.
Conrad, Charles M. Feb. 28, 1850.
Cooper, James. June 29, 1850.
Corwin, Moses B. Apr. 9, 1850.
Crowell, John. June 3, 1850.

Davis, Jefferson. Feb. 13, June 27, 1850.
Davis, John. June 28, 1850.
Dayton, William L. Feb. 23, 1849, Mar. 22, June 11, 1850.
Dickey, Jesse C. June 6, 1850.
Dickinson, Daniel S. Feb. 28 1849, Jan. 17, 1850.
Dimmick, Milo M. June 6, 1850.
Disney, David T. Mar. 13, 1850.
Dix, John A. Feb. 28, 1849.
Donnell, Richard S. Feb. 19, 1849.
Douglas, Stephen A. Mar. 13, June 26, 1850.
Down, Solomon W. Feb. 18, May 22, 1850.
Duer, William. Apr. 10, 1850.
Duncan, James H. June 7, 1850.
Dunham, Cyrus L. June 5, 1850.
Durkee, Charles. June 7, 1850.

Evans, Alexander. Feb. 26, 1849.
Ewing, Andrew. Apr. 18, 1850.

Featherston, Winfield S. Mar. 6, 1850.
Ficklin, Orlando B. Feb. 17, 1849.
Fitch, Graham N. Feb. 14, 1850.

Foote, Henry S. Feb. 23. 1849, May 15, June 27, Aug. 1, 1850.
Fowler, Orin. Mar. 11, 1850.

Gentry, Meredith P. June 10, 1850.
Gerry, Elbridge. May 21, 1850.
Giddings, Joshua R. Mar. 18, 1850.
Gorman, Willis A. Mar. 12, 1850.
Greely, Horace. Feb. 26, 1849.
Green, James S. Apr. 4, 1850.

Hale, John P. Mar. 19, 1850.
Hall, Willard P. Mar. 5, 1850.
Hamilton, William T. June 8, 1850.
Hamlin, Hannibal. Mar. 5, 1850.
Haralson, Hugh A. Aug. 10, 1850.
Harris, Isham G. Apr. 9, 1850.
Harris, Sampson W. June 10, 1850.
Harris, Thomas L. Mar. 25, 1850.
Haymond, Thomas S. May 21, 1850.
Hebard, William. Mar. 14, 1850.
Hilliard, Henry W. Feb. 10, Dec. 12, 1849, Feb. 14, 1850.
Hoagland, Moses. June 5, 1850.
Houston, Sam. Feb. 8, 1850.
Howard, Volney E. June 11, 1850.
Howe, John W. June 5, 1850.
Hubbard, David. June 6, 1850.
Hunter, Robert M. T. Mar. 25, July 18, 1850.

Inge, Samuel W. Feb. 12, 1850.

Jenkins, Timothy. Feb. 17, 1849.
Johnson, Andrew. June 5, 1850.
Johnson, Herschell V. Feb. 28, 1849.
Johnson, James L. Apr. 8, 1850.
Johnson, Robert W. June 7, 1850.
Jones, George W. July 19, Aug. 12, 1850.
Julian, George W. May 14, 1850.

Kaufman, David S. June 10, 1850.
King, Daniel P. May 21, 1850.
King, John A. June 4, 1850.

McClelland, Robert. Feb. 17, 1849.
McClernand, John A. June 10, July 24, 1850.
McDowell, James. Feb. 23, 1849.
McLane, Robert M. Feb. 27, 1850.
McLean, Finis E. June 5, 1850.
McMullen, Fayette. June 8, 1850.
McQueen, John. June 8, 1850.
McWillie, William. Mar. 4, 1850.
Mann, Horace. Feb. 15, 1850.
Marshall, Humphrey. Apr. 3, 1850.
Mason, James M. May 27, 1850.
Meacham, James. May 14, 1850.
Meade, Richard K. June 6, 1850.
Miller, Jacob W. Feb. 21, 1850.
Millson, John S. Feb. 21, 1850.
Morehead, Charles S. Feb. 24, 1849, Apr. 23, 1850.
Morse, Isaac E. Feb. 24, 1849, Mar. 14, 1850.
Morton, Jeremiah. Feb. 6, 1850.
Mullin, Joseph. Feb. 26, 1849.
Murphy, Henry C. Feb. 24, 1849.

Niles, John M. Feb. 28, 1849.

Olds, Edson B. July 24, 1850.
Orr. James L. May 8, 1850.

Palfrey, John G. Feb. 26, 1849.
Parker, Richard. Feb. 28, 1850.
Peck, Lucius B. Apr. 23, 1850.
Phelps, John S. June 8, 1850.
Phelps, Samuel S. Jan. 23, 1850.
Preston, William B. Feb. 7, 1849.
Putnam, Harvey. July 30, 1850.

Richardson, William A. Apr. 3, 1850.
Robinson, John L. Dec. 18, 1848.
Rockwell, John A. Feb. 17, 1849.
Root, Joseph M. Feb. 15, 1850.
Ross, Thomas. Apr. 10, 1850.

Sackett, William A. Mar. 4, 1850.
Savage, John H. May 13, 1850.
Seddon, James A. Jan. 23, 1850.
Seward, William H. Mar. 11, July 2, 1850.
Shields, James. Apr. 5, 1850.
Silvester, Peter H. June 3, 1850.
Smart, Ephraim K. Jan 24, 1849.
Smith, Truman. July 8, 1850.
Soulé, Pierre. May 21, 24, June 24, 1850.
Spaulding, Elbridge G. Apr. 4, 1850.
Stanly, Edward. Mar. 6, 1850.
Stanton, Frederick P. Feb. 13, 1850.
Stanton, Richard H. Mar. 11, 1850.
Starkweather, George A. Feb. 16, 1849.
Stevens, Thaddeus. Feb. 20, June 10, 1850.
Stuart, Charles E. Feb. 26, 1849.

Taylor, John L. June 4, 1850.
Thomas, James H. May 27, 1850.
Thompson, Jacob. June 5, Sept. 7, 1850.
Thompson, John B. Feb. 17, 1849.
Thompson, Richard W. Jan. 25, 1849.
Thurman, John R. June 8, 1850.
Thurston, Samuel R. Mar. 25, 1850.
Toombs, Robert. Feb. 27, 1850.
Turner, Thomas J. Feb. 23, 1849.
Turney, Hopkins L. Mar. 12, 1850.

Upham, William. July 26, 1848, July 1, 1850.

Van Dyke, John. Mar. 4, 1850.

Venable, Abraham W. Feb. 26, 1849, Feb. 19, 1850.

Walker, Isaac P. Mar. 6, 1850.
Wallace, Daniel. Apr. 8, 1850.
Webster, Daniel. Mar. 7, June 27, July 17, 1850.
Wellborn, Marshall J. Feb. 15, June 10, 1850.
Williams, Christopher H. Mar. 18, 1850.
Wilmot, David. May 3, July 24, 1850.
Wilson, James. Feb. 16, 1849.
Winthrop, Robert C. Feb. 21, May 8, 1850.

Yulee, David L. July 23, Aug. 6, 1850.

July 26.   William Upham.
The Compromise Bill. Speech of Hon. W. Upham, of Vermont, in the Senate of the United States, July 26, 1848, On the Bill reported from the Select Committee to establish Territorial Governments in Oregon, New M e x i c o, and California. (Printed at the Congressional Globe Office.)
    7 pp. Caption title.
    Upham saw no necessity for any haste in passing this bill. "The subject is one of momentous importance to the country, and a wise and just disposition of it will require the exercise of all our patience, all our candor, and all our patriotism."
    The speech went into the proceedure and precedence of Congress in organizing and providing territorial governments, and into the slavery question. He contended that all of the territories were then free soil and slavery had no place in them.

Dec. 18.   John L. Robinson.
Speech of Hon. John L. Robinson, of Indiana, on the propriety of establishing Territorial Governments in California and New Mexico. Delivered in the House of Representatives, December 18, 1848. Washington: Printed at the Globe Office. 1848.
    8 pp.
    The speech was reported in the third person.
    Although Robinson was not in favor of the extension of slavery, he considered it prudent not to insist upon any prohibitive bill concerning slavery in the territories recently acquired from Mexico. It would only tend to increase agitation in the Congress between the northern and southern sections, and postpone the action of Congress in the matter of creating governments for these territories. He was of the opinion that the military government under General Persifer F. Smith was quite sufficient in that it gave the people there, better and more protection than they had ever known before.

Jan. 24.   Ephraim K. Smart.
Speech of Mr. E. K. Smart, of Maine, in the House of Representatives, January 24, 1849. Upon the Establishment of Free

Territorial Governments in California and New Mexico.
(Printed at the Office of the Daily Globe.)
   8 pp. Caption title.
   In his speech, Smart made it clear that he was not in favor
of the extension of slavery into territories that were already
free. If slavery were allowed in any of these territories recently
acquired from Mexico it would tempt men into another aggressive war against Mexico for more territorial gain.
   He included descriptions of California, extracted from various sources, on the fertility of the soil, the climate, etc., to
prove that it would support slavery, and extracts from the
"California Star" and the "Californian" on the s l a v e r y
question, both strong in their opposition to slavery, to prove
that it was not wanted. "Thousands of the most respectable
and intelligent young men of the North are now on their way
to California. They have gallantly gone forth, and it is our
duty to establish a free government to protect them."

Jan. 25. Richard W. Thompson.
   The Slavery Question.
   Speech of Mr. R. W. Thompson, of Indiana, in the House
of Representatives, January 25, 1849.
   Printed in the Congressional Globe, no separate seen.
   This was a mild, pacific speech with no Californian interest,
except for one remarkable paragraph: "I do not, Mr. Chairman,
propose to say anything now in reference to the inhibition of
slavery in the territories, which we have acquired by our war
with Mexico, except to remark, . . . that if it had not been for
repeated violations of the Constitution, to which the Abolition
party owes its political existence; if it had not been for the
Abolition party itself, we should have had no Mexican war,
and no Mexican territory. But we have had the war, and we
have got the territory, and what is to be done with it? For my
part, I declare to you, sir, that before I would endanger the
union of these States by the determination of any question
which might arise in the settlement of the controversy between
the North and the South, in reference to New Mexico and
California, I would vote to give it all back, gold mines and

all, to Mexico. Yes, although the gold mines were ten times richer than they are, they should not weigh a feather in the scale, compared with the integrity of the union of these States. But as we cannot give them back, for me, I am in no very great hurry to organize a government for them. I believe gentlemen from all sections had better get cool upon this question before they undertake to do a great deal about it; they are too excited now. There is no sufficient conservatism either in the South or the North. A portion of the North say they will dissolve the Union, unless Congress inhibits slavery in these territories; a portion of the South say they will dissolve the Union if Congress does inhibit slavery there."

Feb. 7. William B. Preston.
California and New Mexico. Speech of Mr. Wm. B. Preston, of Virginia, in the House of Representatives, February 7, 1849, on the formation of a New State out of the Territories of California and New Mexico. Washington: Printed by J. & G. S. Gideon. 1849.
    16 pp.
    Preston offered a bill to establish a state encompassing all of the territory ceded by Mexico under the treaty concluded February 2, 1848, which was to have been called California. The bill called for the erection of the State, with the consent of the people, by the first day of October, 1849, and to be then admitted into the Union.
    The speech was an attempt to recruit support for the bill. There being no reference to slavery in the bill, Preston assumed that a natural course would follow, which according to his logic would give the North a distinct advantage in the colonization. "If a slaveholder emigrate and to take his slaves with him, it is the work of time. His business affairs must be arranged. He is a man of substance and property. He has to collect the last year's hire; he has to collect the proceeds of the sale of his farm, and that is not the work of a moment. But that is not the case with those emigrating there from the North. Many of them are bold, intrepid young men, living on the Atlantic borders, who take ships, and, on the wings

of the wind, or with the velocity of steam, go there before a
slaveholder can turn round. Who from the West go there?
The hardy hunter, who has no home except that bounded by
the heavens and the ocean. He throws his rifle on his shoulder,
and, in the spirit of freedom, reaches it through boundless
forests and trackless prairies."

Feb. 10.   Henry W. Hilliard.
Governments for the New Territories. Speech of Mr. H. W.
Hilliard, of Alabama, in the House of Representatives, February 10, 1849.
   Printed in the Congressional Globe, no separate seen.
   Hilliard had offered the House two bills, in the hope of
settling the territorial question, in the matter of boundaries
and slavery. They met with such violent opposition that he
withdrew them with the intention of offering them as substitute
bills to the Committee on Territories. In this speech he ex-
hibited the plan of each bill and elaborated upon them. The
bills were a boundary adjustment plan, authorizing the people
of California to form a State (which he believed would be a
free State) bounded on the north by Oregon, on the east by
the summit of the Sierra Nevada, and on the south where
that range of mountains touch the sea at 34° 30' north latitude;
"a natural boundary;" a little north of Santa Barbara.
   Texas was to be shorn of her claims above the Missouri
compromise line at 36° 30' and given all the territory below
that line west to the Pacific Ocean, exclusive of the proposed
State of California. Texas was expected to divide herself into
smaller states as did some of the larger states of the original
thirteen. This plan would have allowed slavery to enter all
of the territory acquired from Mexico below 36° 30' excepting
California, which territory had not had slavery since Mexico
had abolished it a quarter of a century before. To salve the
feelings of the North, he gave many square mileage figures,
which went to show that the North was receiving under this
division an excess of some 200,000 square miles.

Feb. 10. Albert G. Brown.
New Mexico and California. Speech of Hon. A. C. Brown,
of Mississippi, in the House of Representatives, February 10,
1849, On the proposition of Mr. Preston, of Virginia, to admit
New Mexico and California as a State; and in reply to Mr.
Hunt on the general policy of the Administration.
7 pp. Caption title.
Preston proposed to admit all of the newly acquired territory as one state, to which Brown objected on the grounds
that it was too large and sparsely settled by a people not
yet possessing rights under our laws and Constitution, and
knowing nothing of our institutions. As to the Americans in
California, he thought there were not more than thirty thousand
gold diggers who would remain there only so long as the gold
digging was profitable.
"Whether I can finally bring myself to vote for any proposition to admit these Territories as States, I cannot now undertake to say."

Feb. 16. George A. Starkweather.
California and New Mexico. Speech of Mr. Starkweather, of
New York, in the House of Representatives, February 16,
1849.
Printed in the Congressional Globe, no separate seen.
This speech was upon the power of Congress to legislate
for the territories, and upon the explosive subject of slavery
in the territories. The territories acquired from the Mexican
war were alluded to only indirectly, but the speech initiated
much of the thought of the many anti-slavery speeches that
were to come later.

Feb. 16. James Wilson.
Speech of Mr. Jas. Wilson, of N. Hampshire, on the political
influence of slavery, and the expediency of permitting slavery
in the territories recently acquired from Mexico: Delivered in
the House of Representatives of the United States, February
16, 1849. Washington: Printed by J. & G. S. Gideon. 1849.
16 pp.

This speech, prompted by an anti-slavery view, gave considerable of the history which led to the passage of the
Ordinance of 1787, the Missouri compromise, and the annexation of Texas. Little was said upon the territorial question,
only that Congress, in Wilson's opinion, has the power, given
to it by the Constitution and precedents, to legislate for the
territories.

Wilson traced the growth of slavery from the first two
dozen slaves who were brought by a Dutch ship to Jamestown
in 1620, to its great political influence in 1849. He called
slavery "a blighting, withering curse upon every country with
which it is infested."

Feb. 16. Henry Bedinger.

The North and the South. Speech of Mr. H. Bedinger, of
Virginia, in the House of Representatives, February 16, 1849.
Printed in the Congressional Globe, no separate seen.

Bedinger saw no proposition for settling the territorial
question offered in the House that he would care to support.
The least objectionable to him was a bill offered by Preston
which provided for a formation into one state of all the Mexican war acquisition. To vest this sovereignty in twenty
thousand adventurers, most of whom are not citizens of the
United States, but "South Americans, Mexicans, Chinese,
mulattoes, free negros, Sandwich Islanders and foreigners
from every part of the globe, is asking, in my poor judgment,
a little too much."

Feb. 17. John B. Thompson.

The Tariff and Slavery Questions. Speech of Mr. J. B.
Thompson, of Kentucky, in the House of Representatives,
February 17, 1849.

Printed in the Congressional Globe, no separate seen.

Thompson asked: "How shall we organize, and what restrictions, if any, as to slavery shall we make in the Territories
of New Mexico and California, recently acquired by the
Mexican war?" It was a year and a half before this was
definitely answered. During the interim, nearly all Congress-

men attempted the answer, each to his own way of thinking. So did Thompson. "The territory is the price of common blood and common treasure. The slave States furnished troops especially volunteers, far beyond their proportionate population, with the non-slave holding States. The very men of the war may wish to emigrate to this territory, locate their bounty lands, take with them slaves acquired by marriage or inheritance, necessary to them by habit and education . . . Congress only can, in my opinion, guaranty [sic] to the people of the fifteen slave States of the Union a right to settle in the territory acquired with slave property."

Feb. 17. Timothy Jenkins.
Slavery in the Territories. Speech of Mr. Jenkins, of New York, on the Mexican Treaty. Delivered in the House of Representatives, February 17, 1849. (Towers, printer.) 16 pp. Caption title.

This speech was an appeal to Congress to provide a government for the territories recently acquired from Mexico, without delay, and to exclude slavery therefrom.

"If an application be made for the admission of California and New Mexico into the Union as States, at once, without having passed through previous discipline under territorial governments, it well becomes us to inquire into the reasons for such extraordinary proceedings."

Feb. 17. Robert McClelland.
Slavery in the New Territories. Speech of Mr. McClelland, of Michigan, in the House of Representatives, February 17, 1849.

Printed in the Congressional Globe, no separate seen.

McClelland took the stand that slavery will come to California and New Mexico unless it is prohibited by legislation. "Maryland, Virginia, North Carolina, Kentucky, Tennessee, Missouri and Arkansas, all slave States, are almost entirely in the same latitudes as Upper California . . . . If slave labor is profitable in these States, why not in California?"

Feb. 17. Samuel A. Bridges.
The Slavery Question. Speech of Mr. Samuel A. Bridges, of
Pennsylvania, in the House of Representatives, February 17,
1849.
Printed in the Congressional Globe, no separate seen.
Bridges, although representing a free state, had no use for
the Wilmot proviso, nor sympathy for any law inhibiting
slavery in the territories. He called the proviso the "Wilmot
agitator," and said "it has done more to disturb the peace and
harmony of the nation, to produce domestic discord, and create
sectional jealousies, than any other subject that has ever been
before an American Congress, save its legitimate parent,
Abolitionism . . .
"Although by birth and education I belong to the North,
and am as much opposed to slavery in the abstract as anyone
from that section of the Union, Yet I unhesitatingly say that
the South has rights as well as the North . . . Our Mexican
possessions are acknowledged to be the joint property of all
the States, in which each has an interest. Then why not
concede the interest and permit it to be enjoyed in the best
way that it can, and in a way that would give satisfaction to
all?"

Feb. 17. Aylett Buckner.
Speech of Aylett Buckner, of Kentucky, on the propriety of
organizing governments for the Territories. Delivered in the
House of Representatives, February 17, 1849. (T o w e r s,
printer.)
16 pp. Caption title.
Buckner gave a good description of the new territories, or
at least what was known about them at the time, using Frémont,
Emory, Abert, Cooke, Johnson, Wilkes and Greenhow as
authorites. The great region extending from Arkansas to the
Colorado River and the Tulare Lakes, as far north as Sa-
cramento was described as "a waste of sand and rock, un-
adorned with vegetation, poorly watered, and unfit, it is
believed, for any useful purposes of life . . . Nature has more
effectually prohibited slavery in New Mexico than can any

legislative enactment of Congress." In reference to the Sa-
cramento and San Joaquin valleys, he said "its general character is barren and unproductive, yet with a fine climate and
the use of irrigation, many parts of it are made to yield
abundantly . . . But this valley can be of little value for agricultural purposes, and must be incapable of sustaining, by its
own agricultural resources, the dense population destined to
inhabit it."

Although he represented a slave State, he was inclined to
believe that slavery would not ever be extended into these
territories. The expense and hardships of transporting slaves
that distance by any of the routes would be a deterring factor.
Then if slavery was to be perpetuated there, it would be
necessary to transport families, and with families only an
average of one in four is able to maintain himself, so the
competition of free labor would be entirely too great.

He gave considerable time to the legal aspect and inter-
national law regarding the inducement of slavery here and
tried to convince his colleagues that Congress cannot legally
change the Mexican law abolishing slavery in these territories,
regardless of their transfer to the United States.

In the printed speech he injects a final paragraph: "To the
voters of the Fourth Congressional District: Gentlemen: I take
this opportunity to announce myself a candidate for re-
election . . ." Needless to say, he was not re-elected.

Feb. 17.   John A. Rockwell.

California and New Mexico. Speech of Mr. John A. Rockwell,
of Connecticut, in Relation to Slavery in the Territories:
Delivered in the House of Representatives of the United States,
February 17, 1849. Washington: Printed by J. & G. S. Gideon.
1849.

16 pp. Printed wrapper.

The speech was opened by reciting resolutions passed by
the Legislature of Connecticut on June 24, 1847. The point
of this was to press an enactment of a provision to exclude
slavery forever from all territories, acquired or annexed.

Rockwell traced the history of the application of the Ordi-

nance of 1787 to the territories of that day, and was surprised
to find that there are now objections in Congress to its application to the territorial bills for New Mexico and California.
Into his speech he injected nearly a dozen excerpts of an
anti-slavery nature from speeches of Madison, Jefferson,
Patrick Henry, and other statesmen, both northern and
southern. He asserted that of the white population in the slave
states, only a small minority are slave-holders; in some states
not a fifth, but only a tenth are slave-holders.

If slavery was to be prohibited in California, it would not
work any great hardship on the majority of Southerners
wanting to emigrate there. "It would be found a far more
effectual exclusion of white men from the North by the admission of slavery in these Territories, than of Southern men
by the prohibition of it."

Feb. 17. Orlando B. Ficklin.
Slavery in the Territories. Speech of Mr. O. B. Ficklin, of
Illinois, in the House of Representatives, February 17, 1849.
Printed in the Congressional Globe; no separate seen.
"If California were now ready with her constitution, I would
be most willing to vote this night, in favor of a bill for her ad-
mission as a State, into this Union."

The admission of Kentucky, Tennessee, Vermont, and
other first States which came into the Union under the new
organization were sufficient precedents to justify Ficklin to
favor the admission of California, whether she came with or
without slavery. He did not believe that the population that
came to us by the treaty with Mexico was fitted to organize
a government, and only that part of California within the
parallels 34° 30' and 41° 30' was of sufficient size and population to be acceptable as a State. The boundaries of this California would seem to have been suggested by Hilliard, in
his speech of February 10.

He gave some little, and fairly accurate description of California. "Agriculture will be pursued to supply the immediate
wants of the inhabitants, but mining must remain the chief
employment of the great body of the people there." A prophecy

which the people of the State have reversed.

Feb. 19. Richard S. Donnell.

Speech of Mr. R. S. Donnell, of N. Carolina, on the Bills to establish a Territorial Government in California and New Mexico: Delivered in the House of Representatives of the United States, February 19, 1849. (J. & G. S. Gideon, printers.) 16 pp. Caption title.

Donnell favored neither of the bills offered for a territorial government for California and New Mexico. He stated that in these territories there are about 150,000 Mexicans and Indians, and some 50,000 emigrants who are not all Americans by any means. "The gold mania has spread over the whole continent of Europe, and England and Germany are sending their thousands as well as Boston and New York." He believed that the territories should be kept under military rule.

Feb. 23. William L. Dayton.

(Speech of Dayton, of New Jersey, in the Senate.)

Printed in the Congressional Globe as part of a debate, with no caption, no separate seen.

Dayton was content in allowing the temporary government to remain in operation in California for a year or two, but proposed to extend the revenue laws of the United States to California and New Mexico.

He had a misconception as to the number of persons either on their way or eventually due to arrive in California. He believed that from 20,000 to 30,000 impermanent gold diggers would arrive by sea and overland from the United States, but from Europe, a very few of the German poor and still fewer of the Irish and English who would have the wherewithall to make the voyage. He said "in the course of one or two years your ships will return laden with more gold diggers than gold dust."

Feb. 23. Henry S. Foote.

(Speech of Foote, of Mississippi, in the Senate.)

Printed in the Congressional Globe as part of a debate, with no caption, no separate seen.

Foote was disposed to risk the temporary concern of California and New Mexico with the President and his counsellors.

He was an adroit statesman with constructive ideas. In debate he was heard as often as, if not more often than anyone in the Senate. He apparently knew of the great stir California was making, and guessed that the influx of people there would alter the picture shortly, and most likely felt that this was not the opportune time to offer anything of consequence.

He became Governor of Mississippi in 1852, and served in that capacity until 1854. In that year he went to California, and remained here until 1858. He was an unsuccessful candidate for United States Senator in 1856, when Broderick defeated him.

Feb. 23. James McDowell.

Speech of Mr. James McDowell, of Virginia, on the formation of Governments of New Mexico and California. Delivered in the House of Representatives, February 23, 1849. Washington: Printed at the Globe Office. 1849.

16 pp.

McDowell offered the argument that even though a fragment of the slave population may move into the new territories it would not add a solitary slave to the population. "Every slave, be it recollected, that is taken to California or to New Mexico, makes one less in some of the States." For this reason it would not alter or improve the representation of slave-holders in Congress. "What harm then, could come of this extension?"

He considered it possible that one day there might be five new slave states, including California and New Mexico, and six or eight free states added to the Union. (He was probably including the Oregon territory in this calculation.)

The speech was long and ran over the alloted hour upon the insistence of those present in the House. In the printing, he labored to report the speech as it was given, but succeeded in part only.

Feb. 23.   Thomas J. Turner.

Slavery in the Territories. Speech of Mr. T. J. Turner, of Illinois, in the House of Representatives, February 23, 1849. Printed in the Congressional Globe, no separate seen.

Turner announced that it was the duty of this Congress to provide territorial governments for California and New Mexico. He said that it would be an injustice to give them a state government at this time. Many people have gone there from all parts of the Union; many for the purpose of amassing a fortune and with the intention of returning; some of these may remain; others have gone there with the intention of remaining permanently; but none have yet houses to shelter them, nor fields to cultivate that they may subsist, and they should not yet be burdened with a state government.

"I am not aware that any large or respectable portion of the citizens of California or New Mexico have petitioned Congress to be admitted as States . . . it would be an act of tyranny in us to force such a condition upon them."

There was not much in the speech upon the subject of slavery in the territories, but he warns the South not to press the discussion, "for I tell you that the arrows of truth, pointed by the force of reason, will penetrate to the very center and foundation of every institution in this Republic that is against natural right and natural reason."

Feb. 24.   John G. Chapman.

Speech of Mr. J. G. Chapman, of Maryland, in the House of Representatives, February 24, 1849, upon the bill to establish a Territorial Government in California, and upon the powers of the Federal Government over slavery in the District of Columbia. (Towers, printer, corner of Louisiana avenue and 6th street.)

16 pp. Caption title.

As the District of Columbia was at one time a part of the State of Maryland, Chapman supported the contention that as Maryland was a slave state, slavery should be acceptable in the District.

He was one of the few Congressmen in an earlier session

who objected to the war with Mexico and the acquisition of territory at its close. "I foresaw the disastrous consequences which might result from the mad spirit of aggression and conquest, by which these provinces were to be annexed to our Republic." Little was said upon the territorial question, only that he would support Preston's bill.

Feb. 24. Henry C. Murphy.

Remarks of Mr. Murphy, of New York, delivered in the House of Representatives, on the 24th of February, 1849. 8 pp. Caption title.

The speech was partly reported, and although it lasted the full alloted hour, the printed speech could be read off in half that time.

Murphy was prone to accept slavery where it already existed as a local institution, but was not in favor of its extension. "If they [slave-holders] wish to immigrate to California they can take the proceeds of their property with them, and can have no object in taking their property with them; unless they expect them to be enhanced in value. Such probably would be the effect. Introducing slaves there would increase the value of those left behind as well as those taken. In this respect therefore an advantage would be enjoyed by the south not participated in by the north, and so far an inequality would be created against the north."

Feb. 24. Charles S. Morehead.

Remarks of C. S. Morehead, of Kentucky, on the necessity of organizing governments for our acquired territories: Delivered in the House of Representatives of the United States, February 24, 1849. Washington: J. & G. S. Gideon; Printers. 1849. 16 pp.

This was a mild pro-slavery speech, proposing that territorial governments be set up in the new territories without any slavery restrictions.

"I am a citizen of a Slaveholding State. My feeling, my sympathies, and all my interests are there . . . I confess that

I do not myself believe that slavery will go there; and, under that conviction, if I were as much opposed to it as any free-soiler in this House, I would not vote for a restriction for a mere triumph of one section of the country over another."

Feb. 24.   Isaac E. Morse.

Speech of Isaac E. Morse, of Louisiana, on the Territorial Bill. Delivered in the House of Representativel, [sic] February 24, 1849. Washington: John T. Towers, Printer. 1849. 8 pp.

This was a pro-slavery speech with outcroppings of venom here and there.

"I am for free soil, but not in that miserable, narrow sectional sense, which makes California and New Mexico free to the inhabitants of every country of every complexion and religion, but prohibits the people of fifteen of these confederated States, sovereigns themselves, from going there, and carrying with them what property they choose." This was the only allusion to California and the other new territories in the entire speech.

Feb. 26.   Abraham W. Venable.

Slavery in the Territories. Speech of Mr. A. W. Venable, of North Carolina, in the House of Representatives, February 26, 1849. In Committee of the Whole . . . on the bill to establish a Territorial Government in California.

Printed in the Congressional Globe, no separate seen.

"When the treaty of peace was ratified, there were supposed to be about 110,000 inhabitants, including Indians, in the ceded territory; a surface equal to at least one-third of the United States, and a population not much exceeding half of the small State of Rhode Island; a population, the larger portion of which are actually savages, and the remainder not highly civilized — particularly ignorant of our social system, and unenlightened as to self-government. For such a people . . . a territorial government is that which circumstances imperiously demand . . . A longer tutelage is indispensible — a time for assimilation must be allowed."

"If we vote for a State government before emigration has

given the southern States a chance, we fix it upon ourselves."

Feb. 26.   Charles E. Stuart.

Speech of Hon. C. E. Stuart, of Michigan, on the bill to establish a Territorial Government for California: Delivered in the House of Representatives, February 26, 1849. Washington: Printed at the Globe Office. 1849.

In Stuart's opinion, Congress has the right and power to legislate for, and to regulate slavery in the territories. He was not in favor of any extension of slavery. If it was now extended, he believed the day would come when the entire Republic of Mexico would be swallowed up by the United States for the additional expansion of slavery. He made no direct mention of California.

Feb. 26.   Thomas S. Bocock.

California and New Mexico. Remarks of Mr. Th. S. Bocock, of Virginia, in the House of Representatives, February 26, 1849.

Printed in the Congressional Globe, no separate seen.

Bocock was content to vote for territorial governments for California and New Mexico if the Wilmot proviso which prohibited slavery, was stricken from the bills. He was not in favor of the substitute bill erecting one state of the entire acquisition, because of the "howling wilderness" that intervenes between the inhabited parts and the difference in the destiny of each. "California has, or shortly will have, commerce with Asia, Europe, the Sandwich Islands, South America and Mexico, but not New Mexico... The people of New Mexico certainly, if not also the Inhabitants of California, are unprepared to take position as the citizens of a sovereign State in the Confederacy."

Feb. 26.   Alexander Evans.

Speech of Mr. Evans, of Maryland, on the Bill to provide a Territorial Government for California: Delivered in the House of Representatives of the United States, February 26, 1849. Washington: Printed by J. & G. S. Gideon. 1849.

16 pp.

The bill referred to in this speech was to provide a territorial government for all of the territory acquired from Mexico, which included all of what is now California, Nevada, Utah, Arizona, a part of New Mexico, Colorado and Wyoming, to be called California. On account of the huge size of the territory, and assuming that it would one day be a free state, Evans was not in favor of the bill.

He estimated the population of California at 40,000 whites, half-breeds, Spaniards, Mexicans and Indians. He put the white population at 8,000 — 10,000 and added: "I am aware that large numbers are supposed to be en route from the United States, but their numbers have been greatly exaggerated."

As a substitute he offered a temporary measure, to last until the end of the first session of the next Congress, which proposed that all of the territory be governed by persons directed by the President.

Feb. 26.   Horace Greely.

Slavery — New Mexico, her boundary. Remarks of Mr. H. Greely, of New York, in the House of Representatives, February 26, 1849, on the Bill to Provide a Territorial Government for California.

Printed in the Congressional Globe, no separate seen.

The speech was comparatively short, and dealt mostly with the Texas — New Mexican boundary question. Greely contended that the people of New Mexico had been free of slavery since it was abolished by Mexico twenty-five years before, and it would be a grave injustice to force them under the domination of slave holding Texas, who was now claiming much of the territory of New Mexico.

In the matter of "admitting or excluding slavery there are two parties interested—the people of the United States and the people of the Territories. Which of these parties desires the extension of slavery? Do the people of California and New Mexico? We know they do not. (I speak, of course of the natives of those lands — the original and permanent people.)"

Feb. 26. Joseph Mullin.

Speech of Mr. Joseph Mullin, of New York, on the Bill to establish a Government for the Territory of California: Delivered in the House of Representatives of the United States, February 26, 1849. Washington: Printed by J. & G. S. Gideon. 1849.

14 pp.

Mullin spent a few minutes berating Congress for not establishing governments for the new territories in this anti-slavery speech.

He did not wish to see these territories set up state governments, nor to admit them as such into the Union, as he said the Southern Representatives ask the Congress to do. The people there are foreign emigrants, unacquainted with our institutions, and a native population that looks upon us as enemies of their religion, oppressors and robbers of their country, and have no feeling in common with us. He deplored the fact that the House passed a bill a few days before extending the revenue laws over California without giving her a government, and that it was here considered a great calamity that England should have the privilege of sending a few dollars worth of her manufactures free of duty, but a small matter that murder was rampant.

Feb. 26. John G. Palfrey.

Speech of Mr. Palfrey, of Massachusetts, on the Bill creating a Territorial Government for Upper California, delivered in the House of Representatives of the United States, February 26, 1849. (n. p. n. d.)

10 pp.

An anti-slavery speech, with no positive ideas upon a government for California or the other territories acquired from Mexico. Palfrey predicted that the Missouri compromise would be employed eventually in these territories.

Feb. 28. John M. Niles.

(Speech of Niles, of Connecticut, in the Senate.)

Printed in the Congressional Globe as part of a debate,

with no caption, no separate seen.

"If we cannot give to those Territories such a government
as they ought to have, such a system as we have given other
Territories, let us not insult them by attempting to subject
them to a despotism. It will be much better to do nothing; let
them alone ... If we neglect to act, the people of California
and New Mexico will establish provisional governments for
themselves. This they have a right to do, and no doubt will do.
By the last accounts from California they had already moved
in this matter."

Feb. 28.   John A. Dix.
Speech of Hon. John A. Dix, of New York, in relation to
Territories acquired from Mexico. Delivered in the Senate
of the United States, February 28, 1849. Washington: Printed
at the Globe Office. 1849.
   14 pp.
Dix was not in favor of the proposition to erect California
and New Mexico, as most of the territory acquired from
Mexico was then known, into one huge state to be called
California. He argued that California was not ready for
statehood, and should have a territorial government (that
should exclude slavery). "Its population is foreign; its interests,
associations, usages, laws and institutions are, in some degree,
alien to our own."

Feb. 28.   Daniel S. Dickinson.
Speech of Mr. Dickinson, of New York, on Establishing a
Government for California. Delivered in the Senate of the
United States, February 28, 1849, (Towers, printer.)
   16 pp. Caption title.
"More than six months have rolled away since the Senate,
after mature deliberation and full debate, passed a bill erecting
efficient civil Governments in the Territories of New Mexico
and California, and sent it to the House of Representatives
for concurrence; where it still reposes upon the table unacted
on."
He stated that Mexico had abolished slavery and that these

territories came to us with laws that prohibit slavery. Most
lawyers in the free states and many in the slave states held
that the laws prohibiting slavery remain until changed by
competent legislation. If slavery is already excluded both by
law and natural impediments, why object to the restriction?
"I object to it because one-half of the states of the Union have
solemnly protested against it, and believe it will be a sentence
of condemnation against them... and I object too because the
true principles of self-government forbid that one community
shall legislate for another."

Feb. 28.   Herschell V. Johnson.
(Speech of Johnson, of Georgia, in the Senate.)
Printed in the Congressional Globe as part of a debate,
with no caption, no separate seen.
"We do not ask you to extend slavery; we say you must
not prohibit it. We say that New Mexico and California are
the common property of the States, and that we have the
same right to carry our slaves there which the New England
man has to carry his spindles or his looms. In this position,
the South feels that she is sustained by the Constitution, and
there she intends to stand."

Mar. 1.   Archibald Atkinson.
Slavery in the Territories. Speech of Mr. A. Atkinson, of
Virginia, in the House of Representatives, March 1, 1849.
Printed in the Congressional Globe, no separate seen.
Atkinson supported the institution of slavery. He said that
at the date of the adoption of the Constitution every state had
slaves. In 1790 New Hampshire, Rhode Island and Connecticut had 3,869, New York, 21,324, New Jersey, 11,423 and
Pennsylvania, 3,737. Some of them were still held in bondage
as late as 1830, then New Jersey had 2,254. "And I pray you,
sir, how did they get rid of them? Not by invoking the aid
of Congress, but by the voluntary act of their owners. They
emancipated some, no doubt; but the greater number were
brought into the market, as they did their cattle, and sold for
the best price that could be obtained. The climate, soil, and

other circumstances of the North, made their labor unprofitable."

He was no friend of the Wilmot proviso, and called it "one of the most absurd political humbugs of the day ... We ask no extension of slavery by law ... But we demand as a right, that you will throw no shackles around us; that we shall not be prohibited from immigrating with our property into any of the new territories... We have acquired a territory which seems to abound in mineral w e a l t h; and its abundance is setting the world agog; people from every quarter are rushing by thousands to acquire its treasure. Our own people find themselves elbowed at every turn by foreigners, who would put them aside, and appropriate to themselves the fruits acquired by the valor and blood of our own brothers... apathy and indifference mark your course, and you hug to your bosoms the Wilmot proviso, though its fangs may reach the very vitals of the body politic."

Dec. 12. Henry W. Hilliard.
Slavery and the Union. Remarks of Mr. H. W. Hilliard, of Alabama, in the House of Representatives, December 12, 1849.
Printed in the Congressional Globe, no separate seen.
Hilliard endeavored to portray the feelings and attitude of the South on the anti-slavery proceedings of the North, more especially on the Wilmot proviso, which he described as "a selfish scheme, which proposes to seize upon and appropriate the entire territory acquired from Mexico," for the exclusive use of free-soilers.

Jan. 17. Daniel S. Dickinson.
Sectional Agitation. Remarks of Hon. D. S. Dickinson, of New York, in the Senate of the United States, January 17, 1850. Upon Mr. Clemens's Resolutions calling for the Instructions of the President concerning California; with a sketch of the Debate of that day. (Printed at the Congressional Globe Office.)
8 pp. Caption title.
Why this was published under the above title is not quite

clear. This was a debate wherein Dickinson's part appears only on two and one-quarter pages of the printed text. An attempt was made to discuss a resolution that requested the President to advise the Senate as to whether or not any person had been appointed as civil or military governor of California since the 4th day of March last. This subject was lost sight of shortly, and the Senate entered upon a period of remarks, criticisms and bickerings, which were not always impersonal.

Dickinson brought out a conception of our Goverment, more or less entertained in that day, which seems to have reversed itself since; "that this Confederacy is a sisterhood of free and independent States associated for a few common purposes, and not a consolidated Federal Government."

Jan. 21, 22.   Lewis Cass.
Territorial Governments. Speech of Hon. Lewis Cass, of Michigan, in the Senate of the United States, January 21 and 22, 1850, on the Government of the Territories, and on the Constitutionality and expediency of the Wilmot Proviso. (Printed at the Congressional Globe Office.)

31 pp. Caption title.

This long-winded discussion of the Wilmot proviso was one of the results of Foote's resolution of December 27: "Resolved, that it is the duty of Congress at this session to establish suitable territorial governments for California, for Deseret and for New Mexico."

Cass disagreed with his constituents in the matter of applying it, and said: "The Wilmot proviso is urged upon the ground of its expediency. It is opposed upon the ground of its unconstitutionality. Those who urge it may well abandon it, when circumstances show that the measure is dangerous in itself, or profitless in its result. Those who oppose it cannot change their conviction of right, . . . is the contest worth the cost? To place this barrier, and as I believe unconstitutional proviso on the statute-book . . . I will take part in no such effort."

Cass was not unaware that on this first day of his speech,

the President's message transmitting the constitution of the newly formed State of California was placed before Congress. In the first few minutes of his speech he said: "And the late proceedings in California to organize a government and the constitution which has been the result, are the best proofs that could be offered of the capacity of the people to lay foundations of their political institutions wisely and justly. What a practical comment is that constitution upon the doubts we have heard expressed in this hall and out of it, respecting the intelligence of these remote territories, and the necessity of restraining them by Congressional legislation."

Jan. 22. Thomas L. Clingman,
of North Carolina, in defence of the South against the Aggressive Movement of the North. Delivered in the House of Representatives, January 22, 1850. (Gideon, & Co., Printers.) 16 pp. Caption title.

If Clingman foresaw the great debate and agitation that was to absorb the attention of Congress for the next six months, or if he did not, he could not have chosen a better subject for his speech to promote the cause of the South, or a more opportune time to deliver it. He aired many of the grievances of the South during the preceding fifty years, leading the way for the many arguments that were to follow from his section of the Nation, on the heel of the President's California message.

He conceived the South as a separate nation of the future, and proposed that no restriction be placed upon slavery at least south of the Missouri compromise line (36° 30' N latitude) in the territories acquired from Mexico. "We would thus, by getting the whole of New Mexico, and having the mountain chain and desert on the west, obtain a proper frontier."

Jan. 23. Samuel S. Phelps.
Slave Question. Speech of Mr. Phelps, of Vermont, in the Senate, January 23, 1850, on the subject of Slavery &c. The Senate having resumed the consideration of the motion to print the Resolutions of the General Assembly of the State

of Vermont on the subject of slavery, which were some time since presented by Mr. Upham (Jan. 8).

Printed in the Congressional Globe, no separate seen.

Phelps maintained that any state had the right to resolve its sentiments, and which should be printed by order of the Senate without any question.

All were anti-slavery resolutions, one instructed the Senators and requested the Representatives from Vermont to use their exertion for a speedy organization of territorial governments for New Mexico and California with a provision forever excluding involuntary servitude.

The application of California for admission and her constitution were known to him, and he used the fact in his argument that nowhere in the world where slavery does not exist, is it wanted.

Jan. 23.   James A. Seddon.

Speech of Hon. J. A. Seddon, of Virginia, on the action of the Executive in Relation to California. Delivered in the House of Representatives, January 23, 1850. Washington: Printed at the Congressional Globe Office. 1850.

12 pp.

Seddon berated President Taylor for sending T. Butler King to California to induce the people there to form a state government and called the action a gross, unconstitutional usurpation of power. "If this action of the Executive be tolerated or sustained, it involves the divesting and stripping the States of this Confederacy without their concurrence, it may be against their will, of the entire sovereignty and rights of eminent domain over this whole Territory of California. They are all transferred and vested in this new State of California, which with enormous proportions, has sprung up into a vigorous existence under the dexterous accouchement of Executive skill."

He advocated strongly that California be remanded to territorial subordination. "The right of sovereignty inherent in the people can only pertain to a previously existing, an organized, or reorganized political community; not to unconnected

masses, casual sojourners, hordes of roaming, unsettled adventurers and gold seekers."

Jan. 30.   Albert G. Brown.
Speech of Mr. A. G. Brown, of Mississippi, in the House of
Representatives, January 30, 1850. On the Subject of Slavery,
and on the Action of the Administration in Relation to California and New Mexico. (Washington: Printed at the
Congressional Globe Office, 1850.)
     8 pp. Caption title.
Brown aired the grievances of the Southern States in a
convincing discussion. He foretold the possibility of disunion,
not so much as a bombastic threat, but as the result of the
uncompromising aggressive action of the North upon the so-
called constitutional rights of the South.
     He was not in favor of the admission of California, and
condemned the President for his activities in that field. He
gave the impression that the people of California had little
to do with the formation of their State convention, but were
induced to act solely upon the suggestion and guidance of
the administration.

Feb. 5, 6.   Henry Clay.
Speech of the Hon. Henry Clay, of Kentucky, on taking up
his Compromise Resolutions on the Subject of Slavery. Delivered in the Senate, Feb. 5th & 6th, 1850. (As Reported by
the National Intelligencer.) New York: Stringer & Towsend,
222 Broadway. 1850.
     32 pp.
The resolutions condensed.
     For the peace and harmony of the Union, to settle contro-
versy arising on the slavery question — therefore resolved:
     1. That California be admitted without any Congressional
interference in the matter of slavery.
     2. That territorial governments be established for the resi-
due of territory acquired from Mexico without any slavery
restrictions.
     3. That the Texas — New Mexico boundary be settled.

4. That it be proposed to Texas that the United States will pay the public debts contracted before annexation in consideration of the relinquishment of the territorial claims against New Mexico.

5. That it is inexpedient to abolish slavery in the District of Columbia.

6. That it is expedient to prohibit the slave trade between the District and other places.

7. That more effectual provision be made in the fugitive slave law.

8. That Congress has no power to obstruct slave trade between the states.

To illustrate the tension that existed in Congress, which Clay believed clearly called for a compromise to salve the feelings and interests of both the North and South, he mentioned that at this same session of Congress it exhausted an entire week to elect a doorkeeper for the House. "It was not as to the man, or the qualities of the man, or who is best adapted to the situation. It was whether the doorkeeper entertained opinions upon certain national measures coincident with this or that side of the House."

Feb. 6. Jeremiah Morton.

The Slave Question. Speech of Mr. J. Morton, of Virginia, in the House of Representatives, Wednesday, February 6, 1850.

Printed in the Congressional Globe, no separate seen.

In voicing what Morton considered the attitude of the South, he said: "The South did not think the Territories would be a proper theatre for slave labor. She did not mean however, to yield the principle, that the precedent might hereafter be urged against her." He drew up a resolution conveying his opinions. "Resolved, that the Territories, the common property of the States of the Union, should be open to all its citizens; that all who emigrate, from each and every State, are equally entitled to legislative protection, for property, which is recognized as such, under the laws of the state from which they may emigrate."

Feb. 8.   Sam Houston.
Speech of Hon. Sam Houston, of Texas, on the subject of
Compromise. In the Senate of the United States, February 8,
1850. (Towers, printer.)
16 pp. Caption title.
Houston claimed that under the Constitution the peoples,
whether of states or territories, have the right to establish
their own governments and enact what laws suit them best,
provided they are in keeping with the requirements of the
Constitution, and that Congress has not the power to impose
any allowances or prohibitions of slavery, or any other subject.
He was in favor of the Missouri compromise line being extended so that states which might be formed south of that line
may adopt slavery as a legal institution.
This was a mild pro-slavery speech with some attempt to
pacify, although at this time the hornet's nest had hardly yet
stirred.
There was some allusion to the Texas boundary question,
but none to a government for California or New Mexico.

Feb. 11, 12.   John M. Berrien.
Slavery in the Territories. Speech of Mr. Berrien, of Georgia,
in the Senate, February 11 and 12, 1850. The Senate having
resumed the consideration of the Compromise Resolutions
offered by Mr. Clay on the 25th of January.
Printed in the Congressional Globe, no separate seen.
In this speech, Berrien did not concern himself with arguments on the admission application of California. He gave his
conclusion on that subject by addressing the "gentlemen of
the South, it is not Congress that has prevented you from going
to California and establishing your institutions there; it is the
people of California themselves. California has filled up by
emigration from the free States, while the people of the South
have been prevented from emigrating by the doubt that has
been thrown upon their rights to take with them their slave
property."

Feb. 12 and 20.   Lewis Cass.

Remarks of Mr. Cass, of Michigan, on the dissolution of the
Union, and the Constitution of California. In the Senate of
the United States, February 12 and 20, 1850. On the former
day, upon the presentation of a petition by Mr. Hale, of New
Hampshire, asking the peaceable dissolution of the Union;
and on the latter day, upon the motion to refer the President's
Message, transmitting the Constitution of California. (Towers,
printer.)

8 pp. Caption title.

The speech of February 12 was spontaneous and short,
occupying less than three pages of the eight. "This petition
asks us to dissolve the Union. I shall vote for rejecting it; and
if there were any other mode by which our indignation at
such a wicked and foolish proposition could be more power-
fully expressed, I should adopt it with pleasure."

The speech of February 20 was an attempt to vindicate
and clarify some of his earlier remarks. "As I have said, I laid
down four propositions or opinions, if you please, in my
Nicholson letter. The first, that the Wilmot Proviso was
unconstitutional; second that slavery, having been abolished
by the Mexican Government, did not exist in the territory
then held by our arms; third, that slavery would not go there,
as well on account of natural and geographical obstacles, as
on account of the feelings of the people, who were and might
be there; and fourth, that organized communities, exercising
the powers of Government, whether State or Territorial, had
alone the right of determining this question for themselves."

Feb. 12.   Samuel W. Inge.

California and New Mexico. Speech of Mr. S. W. Inge, of
Alabama, in the House of Representatives, February 12, 1850.
On the policy of the Administration in reference to the Terri-
tories of California and New Mexico.

Printed in the Congressional Globe, no separate seen.

Inge gave no credit to the people of California for forming
a state government, instead he blamed the Chief Executive
and his agents. The result weakened the solidarity of the

South, which stood as a body against the Wilmot proviso being applied to the territories, substituting, as he called it, the California proviso. This saved the administration the embarrassment of having to declare itself on the slavery question in California. It put the South in the difficult position of having to decide against the admission of California and abrogating its cherished theory of states-rights and self-determination, or accept her as a free state, without the admission of a slave state to hold the balance.

Feb. 13, 14.   Jefferson Davis.

Slavery in the Territories. Speech of Mr. Davis, of Mississippi, in the Senate, February 13 and 14, 1850. The Senate having, as in Committee of the Whole, proceeded to the consideration of the resolutions submitted by Mr. Clay on the subject of slavery in the Territories.

Printed in the Congressional Globe, no separate seen.

Davis said that Clay, who was supposed to be representing those southern interests which were at stake, surrenders the whole claim of the South. In the case of California, he said: "we are bound to accept such terms as the inhabitants of the Territory possessing it, under such circumstances, shall think fit to dictate to us. That the will of the conglomerated mass of gold-hunters, foreign and native, is to be taken as the decree of nature, and to be held authoritative for the exclusion of citizens of the United States from equal privileges which the Constitution declares, and was established to secure."

He saw no gain or advantages to the South in the other resolutions of Clay's compromise.

If the United States was to abide by the Mexican law prohibiting slavery in these territories, then there was no sufficient reason why other Mexican laws should not also stand. There were about sixty articles of ordinary commerce that were prohibited by Mexico, including cotton, cotton fabrics, salt, tobacco, coarse woolen cloths, grain, most kinds of leather, and many manufactured articles, which should also be prohibited along with slaves by the United States. There was no place for Protestantism in Mexico, should this also be forbiden?

"But we at the South are an agricultural people, and require an extended territory. Slave labor is a wasteful labor, and therefore requires a still more extended territory than would the same pursuits if they could be prosecuted by the more economical labor of white men."

Feb. 13.   Frederick P. Stanton.
California and New Mexico. Speech of Hon. F. P. Stanton, of Tennessee, in the House of Representatives, February 13, 1850. Upon the question concerning the admission of California as a State, and the circumstances which led to the formation of the Constitution of California. (Printed at the Congressional Globe Office.)
7 pp. Caption title.
Stanton was convinced that President Taylor through his agent, T. Butler King, directed the forming of the California constitution with its anti-slavery clause. He summed it up by saying; "what the people of California have done is strictly revolutionary, and the President of the United States has been virtually at the head of the revolution."
He concerned himself over the North — South balance of representation in Congress, and was not favorable to the admission of California as a state. This was a vehement, uncompromising speech, the tone of which is illustrated by his remark: "In this state of exasperated feeling, how long can you expect to maintain a union? . . . I shall be prepared to go with the southern people in whatever they may determine — even though it be to abandon the Union."

Feb. 14.   Graham N. Fitch.
The Slave Question. Speech of Mr. Graham N. Fitch, of Indiana, in the House of Representatives, Thursday, February 14, 1850.
Printed in the Congressional Globe, no separate seen.
The speech was not directly upon the California question. In no conciliatory terms, Fitch discussed the speeches of

several Southern Representatives on that subject, but more
particularly on the Wilmot proviso and the extension of
slavery into the new territories.

Feb. 14. Henry W. Hilliard.
Speech of Mr. H. W. Hilliard, of Alabama, on the President's
Message, in relation to the Government of the Territory
acquired from Mexico by the treaty of Guadalupe Hidalgo.
Delivered in the House of Representatives of the United
States, February 14, 1850. Washington: Gideon & Co.,
Printers. 1850.
  8 pp.
Hilliard was not in accordance with the President's recommendation that California be admitted and the people of the
residue of the territory acquired from Mexico work out their
own government, "Slavery excluded from California by the
constitution of that State would leave no field for any further
exertion on the part of its enemies, but they would enter upon
the task of excluding it from the remaining territories."
He conceded that the people have the right to determine
their state government, but claimed that the New York
Volunteers, a regiment raised in the interior of New York,
went to California with the purpose of colonizing and establishing a free soil territory. "I prefer to settle this question by
adopting the Missouri compromise line . . . If California is to
come into the Union, let the State be admitted with the
Missouri compromise line for its southern boundary, and let
us settle the whole question upon that line."

Feb. 15. Arthur P. Butler.
Remarks of Hon. A. P. Butler, of South Carolina, on the
proposition to admit California as a State into the Union.
Delivered in the Senate of the United States, February 15,
1850. Washington: Printed at the Congressional Globe
Office. 1850.
  7 pp.
Butler found no particular fault with the constitution of
California, even with its anti-slavery clause, but in repre-

senting a slave-holding state was obliged to object to her admission. He pointed out that the boundaries elected by the
Californians, because they were not designated by Congress
are unconstitutional and found no precedent of the kind. He
questioned the status of the twelve or thirteen thousand who
voted on the constitution. "Were they free white men? Were
they Mexicans of Spanish blood? Were they such Mexicans
as were recognized as capable of becoming citizens under the
terms of the treaty? . . . No state in this Union has come into
it without Congress having previously taken a census of its
inhabitants."

Feb. 15. Joseph M. Root.
California and New Mexico. Speech of Hon. Joseph M. Root,
of Ohio, in the House of Representatives, February 15, 1850.
In Committee of the Whole on the state of the Union, on the
Resolution referring the President's Message to the appropri-
ate Standing Committees. (Printed at the Congressional Globe
Office.)

7 pp. Caption title.

"I shall first notice his [President Taylor's] recommendation respecting California; and I beg leave here to say that
perhaps under other circumstances I should feel disposed to
criticise some of the proceedings which led to the formation
of a constitution for California and her application to be
admitted into the Union as a State. I might think that a better
boundary might be prescribed for her on the east. Yet as
things now stand I am perfectly willing, ready, and desirous
to have her recognized as a State with her boundaries as they
are."

He clearly brought forth an accusation against the Southern
members of an earlier Congress, that was alluded to from
time to time in a few of the contemporary speeches, by
pointedly asking the Chairman, Linn Boyd, of Kentucky; "You
were a member of the 29th and 30th Congresses, and an
ardent supporter of the Mexican war. Let me ask you, sir,
what was that war begun and prosecuted for? Was it not for
territory? and was it not obvious from the beginning that it

would only result in the acquisition of territory? and was it
not just as obvious that when the territory should be acquired,
the strife that we now have must come? Were you not warned,
over and over again that the attempt would be made to exclude
slavery from it, and that it would be persisted in to the end?
Yes; but you and your friends sneered at the warning. You
confidently expected to be able to appropriate the whole or
the greater part of it to slavery . . . Her [Mexico's] mines
and her valleys now and ever will hold out almost irresistable
temptations to our southern brethren to provoke war with her."

Feb. 15. Marshall J. Wellborn.
The Slave Question. Speech of Mr. M. Wellborn, of Georgia,
in the House of Representatives, Friday, February 15, 1850.
Printed in the Congressional Globe, no separate seen.
In this speech Welborn offered two resolutions to be held
in abeyance for a future time.
1. Resolved, that California be admitted into the Union
with her present constitution, restricting her southern boundary to the parallel of 36 degrees and 30 minutes north latitude.
He spent little time discussing this resolution, except to
mention that the people that voted upon the constitution of
California were in part aliens to our laws, language and religion, and not clothed with the elective franchise, and only
in part members of these States. "But on whose territory do
they propose to exert this authority of self-government?" He
objected to the largeness of the state within the proposed
boundaries.
The second resolution was elaborated upon at more length.
It proposed a bill to organize a territory for the southern
portion of California, New Mexico and Deseret, prohibiting
slavery north of 36° 30' and allowing it south, until the
adoption of state constitutions by the people thereof.

Feb. 15. Horace Mann.
Speech of Horace Mann, of Massachusetts, on the subject
of Slavery in the Territories, and the consequences of a Dissolution of the Union. Delivered in the United States House of

Representatives, February 15, 1850. Boston: Redding and
Company, 1850.
35 pp. Printed wrapper.

Mann answered some of the speeches of Southern Representatives; showing their about-face the moment California
asked for admission as a free state, in the matter of the creed
that a people in forming a state have the right to adopt the
government that suits them; the objection to the large size
of California from the same Congressmen who were most
strenuous for the admission of Texas.

He proceeded to argue against the importation of slaves
into California and into any of the territories. Each slave
state has its own laws governing slavery; in Delaware, for
instance, it is a penal offence to sell a slave to a notorious
slave dealer; in Georgia it is illegal to import slaves for sale;
then how can a Georgian import slaves into California when
the laws of his own state forbid it? In South Carolina the
ownership of ten slaves constitutes a property qualification
for being a member of the legislature. Can this be carried to
California? Not any more than could the Chinese practice of
infanticide, or the South Sea Island practice of cannibalism.

This was one of the most able, concise and logical speeches
of the time, without any element of compromise. About half
of the speech was given over to a caustic discussion on the
possibility of a dissolution of the Union and civil war, which
should have discouraged the leaders of the Southern States,
and possibly did for another ten years.

Feb. 18, 19. Solomon W. Downs.
Speech of Mr. Downs, of Louisiana, on the Compromise Resolutions of Mr. Clay. In Senate, February 18 and 19, 1850.
16 pp. Caption title.

Downs said that the constitution of California was not an
expression of the people there, but was concocted elsewhere
and brought into California. He went to great lenghths in his
attempt to prove it. The speech seems to be the argument of
a rather disgruntled pro-slavery man who foresaw a preponderance of square mileage becoming free soil. He did not

favor the compromise resolutions, nor the admission of California.

Feb. 19.   Abraham W. Venable.
President's Message — California. Speech of Hon. A. W. Venable, of N. Carolina, in the House of Representatives, February 19, 1850. In Committee of the Whole on the state of the Union, on the Resolution referring the President's Message to the appropriate Standing Committees.
15 pp. Caption title.
In this able and adroit speech, the references to California were but slight. "I do not now propose to do more than make a reference to this subject. At another time when the Executive communication shall have been printed, and the whole matter placed before us, I shall express my views in relation thereto."
He was convinced that the President meddled in California and induced a government to be established with an anti-slavery clause, and deplored "this whole transaction."

Feb. 19.   Lewis D. Campbell.
Southern Aggression — The Purposes of the Union — and Comparative Effects of Slavery and Freedom! Speech of Mr. L. D. Campbell, of Ohio, in the House of Representatives, Tuesday, February 19, 1850.
Printed in the Congressional Globe, no separate seen.
Campbell made this speech with the intention of doing his utmost to keep slavery out of all of the territories. He put himself on record as being in favor of the admission of California with the slavery prohibition in her constitution, and a territorial law for New Mexico embracing the same prohibition.

Feb. 20.   Thaddeus Stevens.
Speech of Mr. Thaddeus Stevens, of Pennsylvania, In the House of Representatives, on the Reference of the President's Annual Message. Made in Committee of the Whole, February 20, 1850. (Printed and for sale by Buell & Blanchard.)
8 pp. Caption title.
This was an anti-slavery speech, with no direct reference

to the admission of California. It was aimed against the expansion of slavery into the territories.

Feb. 20. William V. N. Bay.

President's Message — Slavery — California. Speech of Mr. W. V. N. Bay, of Missouri, in the House of Representatives, Wednesday, February 20, 1850.

Printed in the Congressional Globe, no separate seen.

Bay stated that no Southerner could oppose the admission of California on the grounds that she prohibited slavery without being inconsistent. Her constitution will compare favorably with any state. It was adopted by the unanimous vote of her convention, which consisted of forty delegates — thirty-six Americans, of whom twenty came from the free states and sixteen from the slave states.

"I should have been better pleased if her constitution had been silent upon the subject of slavery . . . I shall vote to curtail her boundaries . . . But California must come into the Union."

Feb. 21 and 25. Jacob W. Miller.

Speech of Mr. Miller, of New Jersey, on the propositions to Compromise the Slavery Question, and the Admission of California into the Union. Delivered in the Senate of the United States, February 21, 1850. Washington: Printed by Jno. T. Towers. 1850.

32 pp.

Miller, in his pleading for the admission of California mentioned how the Californians were divided as to representation of Northern and Southern States: Fifty thousand were from Northern States and thirty thousand from Southern States. At the constitutional convention there were fourteen native Californians, nineteen from Northern States and fifteen from Southern States. When the constitution was voted upon there were thirteen thousand votes in favor and eight hundred and eleven against it, including only eighteen that were from below the Missouri compromise line if it had been extended to the Pacific Ocean. In the newly formed legislature there

were two native Californians and five members from Southern
States in the Senate of sixteen, and in the Assembly of thirty
six, one native Californian, and seventeen from Southern
States.

Feb. 21. Robert C. Winthrop.

Speech of the Hon. R. C. Winthrop, of Mass., on the President's Message; delivered in Committee of the Whole in the
House of Representatives of the United States, February 21,
1850. Washington: Printed by Gideon & Co., 1850.

16 pp.

Winthrop stated that he was ready to vote for the admission of California, and that he would not sanction any
action which might induce slavery into the territories. This
was stated without argument or embellishment, and beyond
this, nothing was said of any national importance or interest.
The so-called speech was but a self-vindication of his current
position, and a re-hash of a session held nearly four years
earlier. Why this speech was considered worth printing is
not obvious.

Feb. 21. William H. Bissell.

The Slave Question. Speech of Hon. Wm. H. Bissell, of
Illinois, in the House of Representatives, February 21, 1850.
In Committee of the Whole on the state of the Union, on the
Resolution referring the President's Message to the approriate
Standing Committees.

8 pp. Caption title.

This speech was upon the attitudes of Southern Representatives toward the Union and the North, rather than upon
"The slave question." He took particular exception to the
speeches of Brown of Mississippi and Clingman of North
Carolina, from which he quoted and answered in no uncertain
terms. There were only two short allusions to California, both
induced by the remarks of Brown, who stated that the admission of California should be resisted, first by vote, or lastly
by force. Bissell said; "Alas for the 100,000 men already
there, or on their way thither, from whom California is to be

taken by force, and held by armed occupation, that slavery
may be introduced there against their will." Brown stated that
the admission of California was "unwise, insulting to the
South, despicable." Bissell told the House that a slave-holding
President with a Cabinet, the majority of which were slave-
holders, sent to California, (Thomas Butler) King, a slave-
holder, who returns, "bringing as trophies two Southern
men — one a Mississippian [Gwin] and the other a South
Carolinian [Frémont] — (and both slave-holders, I believe)
whom our Southern President desires to introduce into the
Senate . . . and thereupon our southern friends declare that if
this infamous measure of 'northern aggression' is carried out
the Union shall be dissolved and the North held responsible!"

Feb. 21 and 26.   John S. Millson.
Speech of Hon. J. S. Millson, of Virginia, in the House of
Representatives, February 21 and 26, 1850, In Committee of
the Whole on the state of the Union, on the Resolution referring the President's Message to the appropriate Standing
Committees. (Printed at the Congressional Globe Office.)
   7 pp. Caption title.
   This was a pro-slavery speech aimed at Northern Representatives, but most particularly aimed at parts of Horace
Mann's speech. Millson wanted slavery allowed in California
and the other territories acquired from Mexico. "Let them
[Northerners] reflect upon the probable consequences of
penning up the slaves within a narrow limit — their great
increase in number the lessened demand for their labor — the
diminished inducement to good treatment — the war between
the two races likely to spring up — and let them ask themselves
the question, whether it would not be better to extend slavery
than restrict it — by a massacre of slaves."

Feb. 27.   Robert Toombs.
Speech of Mr. R. Toombs, of Georgia, in the House of Representatives, February 27, 1850, in Committee of the Whole on
the state of the Union, on the President's Message comunicat-
ing the Constitution of California. (Gideon & Co., Printers.)

8 pp. Caption title.

A pro-slavery argument culminating in a demand for "equal participation in the whole country acquired, or a division of it between the North and the South." (To allow slave-holders to take slaves anywhere into the new territories, or to extend the Missouri compromise line to the Pacific). He accused the North of now wanting to repudiate the compromise after gaining two-thirds of Louisiana, a portion of Texas, and all of Oregon.

Feb. 27.   Robert M. McLane.

Admission of California. Speech of Hon. R. M. McLane, of Maryland, in the House of Representatives, February 27, 1850. In Committee of the Whole on the state of the Union, on the President's Message communicating the Constitution of California. (Printed at the Congressional Globe Office.)

8 pp. Caption title.

McLane made it plain that he would vote for the admission of California if some compromise was made. He suggested that California include all of the Pacific Coast and be admitted as a free state, and that Texas be extended to the eastern boundary of California, thus there would be one huge free state and another huge slave state, both to be later subdivided into smaller states as Congress saw fit.

The printed speech is not in his own words, but reported in the third person.

Feb. 28.   Richard Parker.

Speech of Hon. Richard Parker, of Virginia, on the President's Message in relation to California. Delivered in the House of Representatives, Thursday, February 28, 1850. Washington: Printed at the Congressional Globe Office. 1850.

8 pp.

The speech was mostly upon the constitutionality of slavery, and the power of Congress to exclude it from the territories.

In one paragraph only, near the end of the speech, did Parker make any reference to California. He mentioned that an attempt was made "But the other day" to force a bill

through the House instructing one of the committees to report
a bill for the admission of California, without debate, and
prohibiting that committee from connecting any provisions
for governments for the other territories therewith. He found
her boundaries to be very objectionable and her sea-coast too
long, "extending over nine hundred miles, reaching as far as
from Boston to Savannah."

Feb. 28.   Charles M. Conrad.

Speech of Hon. C. M. Conrad, of Louisiana, on the President's
Message in relation to California. Delivered in the House of
Representatives, Thursday,, February 28, 1850. Washington:
Printed at the Congressional Globe Office. 1850.

  8 pp.

Conrad was not disposed to view the newly acquired territory in the same light as other Southerners. He was of the
opinion that slavery, regardless of any man made laws will
not thrive in regions where nature is inhospitable to it. Using
Emory's "Reconnoissance" as his authority, he said; "I must
candidly confess that I have long since come reluctantly to the
conclusion, that nature has decided this question against the
South . . . I would willingly give Mexico twice as much to
take back the country as it cost us. . . . The only portion of
this territory that we did need, was an harbor or two on the
Pacific, which might have been purchased at a trifling cost,
and the government of which would not have exposed the
country to all the agitation and excitement which this question
has produced.

In my opinion, sir, the people of California have acted
wisely in preferring a government, however irregularly consti-
tuted, to no government at all, and the President, in affording
every encouragement to the accomplishment of this object,
has done no more than his duty." But owing to the irregularities, the convention that framed the California constitution
not being authorized by Congress, the lack of a census, he
would not vote for her admission as a separate bill, but would
vote for a compromise bill of "honorable settlement", which
included the admission of California.

Mar. 4. John C. Calhoun.
Speech of Mr. Calhoun, of South Carolina, on the Slavery Question. Delivered in the Senate of the United Estates, March 4, 1850. (Towers, printer, corner of Sixth street and Louisiana avenue.)
16 pp. Caption title.
"I have, Senators, believed from the first that the agitation of the subject of slavery would, if not prevented by some timely and effective measure, end in disunion."
After this opening remark he proceeded to give some of the causes of the agitation. According to the 1790 census the population of the Northern States was 1,977,899 and the Southern States was 1,952,072, which gave the North but a small preponderance in the House and in the electoral college. The 1840 census showed 9,728,820 in the North and 7,334,437 in the South, and he knew that the 1850 census would further disparage the equilibrium existing between the North and South. "Had this destruction been the operation of time, without the interference of the Government, the South would have not reason to complain; but such was not the fact." Through Government legislation (the ordinance of 1787 and the Missouri compromise) the North has appropriated 1,764,023 square miles of territory, including States, leaving the South with 609,023 square miles. If the North should succeed in monopolizing the newly acquired territories there will be 2,373,046 square miles from which the South will be excluded.
Another factor irksome to the South was a "system of revenue and disbursements, by which an undue proportion of the burden of taxation has been imposed upon the South and an undue proportion of its proceeds appropriated to the North . . . . But while these measures were destroying the equilibrium between the two sections, the action of the Government was leading to a radical change in its character by concentrating all the power of the system in itself."
He brought forth the argument that C a l i f o r n i a was conquered by the United States and not by adventurers as was Texas, therefore it is the right of Congress to provide a government, and not the right of the individuals to form a

constitution and a state. "What they have done is revolutionary and rebellious in its character, anarchical in its tendency,
and calculated to lead to the most dangerous consequences....
In this respect California stands alone, without usage, or a
single example to cover her case ... remand her back to the
territorial condition."
Although Calhoun later entered into some of the debates,
this was the last speech of this great statesman. He died
March 31, 1850.

Mar. 4.   William A. Sackett.
Shall Slavery be Extended? Speech of Hon. W. A. Sackett,
of New York, in the House of Representatives, March 4,
1850, In Committee of the Whole on the state of the Union,
on the President's Message communicating the Constitution
of California. (Printed at the Congressional Globe Office.)
    8 pp. Caption title.
    This was a speech against the extension of slavery into any
of the territories. The references to California were only slight,
with none to her constitution, nor her application for admission.

Mar. 4.   John Van Dyke.
Speech of Mr. John Van Dyke, of New Jersey, delivered in
the House of Representatives of the U. States, March 4, 1850,
on the subject of slavery, and in vindication of the North
from the charges brought against it by the South. Washington: Gideon and Co., Printers. 1850.
    14 pp.
    "If the South is to be believed, the North, as a people and
as States, are a set of Goths and Huns, Alarics and Attilas
— robbers, cut-throats, and constitution breakers, whose
great object is to free the slaves, burn the dwellings, cut the
throats of the masters, and dishonor the wives and daughters
of the South.
    If a territory desire slavery within its limits, and if it be a
'great, social, civil, political, and religious blessing — a
blessing to the slave and a blessing to the master;' if it tend

to make a country great and strong, and prosperous and happy; and if it tend to develop their resources, to increase enterprise, industry and labor — then, if we think so, let them have it. But if, on the contrary, we believe it to be a great evil, a great moral wrong, a blight and a curse upon every country where it exists — if it hinder emigration, [sic] if it depress enterprise, if it discourage industry and labor, by making it disreputable for a white man to work — and, above all, if the people to be affected are deadly hostile to it, why, I ask, in the name of all that is just and reasonable, why should we either put it upon them or allow it to go there, if we can prevent it?"

Mar. 4. William McWillie.

Permanency of Free Institutions. Speech of Hon. W. Mc-Willie, of Mississippi, in the House of Representatives, March 4, 1850. In Committee of the Whole on the state of the Union, on the President's Message communicating the Constitution of California. (Printed at the Congressional Globe Office.)

8 pp. Caption title.

"My mind is deliberately made up to the conviction that the South ought not to take less than the Missouri compromise." He did not specifically mention California, but it is assumed that she was included.

"We do not propose to make any freeman a slave, nor do we propose to open the African slave trade. All that we ask is that the master and his slave, may be permitted to enter the common territory of the Union." "If California and New Mexico are not suited to slave labor, every slave carried there would soon become a free man."

Mar. 5. Hannibal Hamlin.

Speech of Hon. Hannibal Hamlin, of Maine, on the proposition to Admit California as a State into the Union. Delivered in the Senate of the United States, March 5, 1850. Washington: Printed at the Congressional Globe Office. 1850.

14 pp.

Hamlin's discussion is based on the principle that Congress

has not the right to establish a state government, the people alone have that inherent right and Congress can only admit a state upon application if it qualifies.

Regarding the charges that there was interference by the President in the formation of California by urging the people to establish their government, he said that King was the first person to arrive there after the inauguration of Taylor, and the time of arrival was one day after General Riley's proclamation fixed the time of meeting at the very same time already fixed by the people themselves at their own primary meetings, so it is quite impossible to say that the Administration suggested any preliminary steps in the formation of the State government.

Mar. 5.   E. Carrington Cabell.

The Slave Question. Speech of Hon. E. C. Cabell, of Florida, in the House of Representatives, March 5, 1850, In Committee of the Whole on the state of the Union, on the President's Message communicating the Constitution of C a l i f o r n i a. (Printed at the Congressional Globe Office.)

8 pp. Caption title.

"What do we of the South ask? We have fought for, and are to pay for, the territory acquired from Mexico, and we merely ask that we may not be excluded from its enjoyment. We cannot go, unless you permit us to take our property with us; and we contend that Congress, with its limited powers, can not, and with any powers, should not exclude us."

There was no allusion to the admission of California.

Mar. 5, 1850.   Willard P. Hall.

Speech of Hon. Willard P. Hall, of Missouri, on the Admission of California. Delivered in the House of Representatives, Tuesday, March 5, 1850. Washington: Printed at the Congressional Globe Office. 1850.

13 pp.

"I not only say that the people of California have acted properly, and that we may properly admit them into the Union, but that it is our duty so to admit them ... We should remember, that the American citizens, resident there, had revolutionized all the country around the Bay of San Francisco, and north thereof, before we attemped to take possession of it . . . but for our interference, California would at this time, have been an independent state."

Hall put before the House his conviction that the peoples of any state or territory had, under the Constitution, the right to govern themselves with any legal provisions they chose, without the interference of Congress. He favored the admission of California and the forming of a territorial government for the residue of the Mexican acquisition, without any restrictions impeding slavery.

Mar. 6, 8. Isaac P. Walker.

Compromise Resolution. Speech of Mr. Walker, of Wisconsin, in the Senate, March 6, 1850.

Printed in the Congressional Globe, no separate seen.

After the opening paragraph this speech deteriorated into a general debate upon the extension of slavery into the territories. It was interrupted by the great speech of Webster on March 7th, and concluded March 8th.

During the course of this much interrupted speech, and it was interrupted some fifty odd times, Walker offered tables to prove that the expansion of slavery beyond its then present limits was needless. Of the 674,613,895 acres in the slave states there were 394,613,895 acres unoccupied, and which exceeded the entire acreage of the free states by 103,836,285.

He contended that if slavery, which was a local institution, was allowed to be taken into California and New Mexico, then other local institutions — New York with her banking property and other states with their lotteries — should have the same privilege.

Mar. 6. Winfield S. Featherston.

Speech of Hon. Winfield S. Featherston, of Mississippi, on the President's Message in relation to California. Delivered in the House of Representatives, March 6, 1850. Washington: Printed at the Congressional Globe Office. 1850.

8 pp.

Featherston was opposed to the admission of California
on the grounds that Congress alone has the power to authorize
a state constitution; that no territorial pupilage had been
imposed; and that a large portion of the population was not
permanent, some had gone on an observation tour, others to
gather gold for a season and then leave. His real objection,
of course, was to the anti-slavery constitution.

Mar. 6. Edward Stanly.

Speech of Edward Stanly, of N. Carolina, exposing the causes
of the slavery agitation. Delivered in the House of Representatives, March 6, 1850. (Gideon & Co., Printers.)

16 pp. Caption title.

Stanly did not agree with all of his Southern brethern
House members. He discussed portions of their several
speeches to show that their vehemence in promoting the cause
of slavery had done as much to stir agitation on the slavery
question as any of their Northern brethern had. He stood on
the premise that the people of any section of this country,
including California and New Mexico, have the Constitutional
right to self-determination.

Mar. 7. Daniel Webster, of Massachusetts.

Speech of Hon. Daniel Webster, on Mr. Clay's Resolutions,
in the Senate of the United States, March 7, 1850. Washington: Printed by Gideon & Co., 1850.

64 pp. Printed wrapper.

Same. Boston: Redding and Company, 1850.

39 pp. Printed wrapper.

Same with variant wrapper. "As revised and corrected by
permission, for the Daily Atlas, March 11th."
Speech of the Hon. Daniel Webster, upon the subject of
Slavery; delivered in the Senate of the United States on
Thursday, March 7, 1850. Boston: Hotchkiss & Company.
Office of "The Yankee Nation," 13 Court St., 1850.

36 pp. Title on wrapper. Portrait.
Speech of Mr. Webster on Mr. Clay's Resolutions. Delivered

in the Senate of the United States, March 7, 1850. Gideon &
Co., Printers.

15 pp. Caption title.

2nd edition, same.

A great speech of a great orator, that rattled every stone
in the Capitol. It is not as flowery as many other speeches,
but its context, and no doubt its delivery by this dominant
personality, caused it to be acclaimed as the most outstanding
at this Congress.

He dwelt mostly upon the subject of slavery, not in the
aggravating way of abolitionists, but treating it with an
unbiased point of view, recognizing its constitutionality where
it existed. He stated that in the new territories, particularly
New Mexico, any man made prohibition is unnecessary, as a
higher law, the law of Nature has made it impossible for it to
thrive here. He discussed some of the complaints and exasper-
ations of both the North and the South, and ends this portion
of his speech by observing that in 1832 public opinion in the
South, particularly in Virginia, was not unagreeable to the
gradual abolition of slavery, but in 1835 abolition societies
became active in the North against Southern slavery. "Well,
what was the result? The bonds of the slaves were bound
more firmly than before; their rivets were more strongly
fastened."

On the California question he made no decided stand. He
merely reviewed some of the circumstances which led to the
establishment of a state government, and the framing of a
constitution. "This constitution, sir, contains an express prohi-
tion against slavery, or involuntary servitude in the State of
California. It is said, and I suppose truly, that the members
who composed that convention, some sixteen were natives,
and had been residents in the slaveholding States, about
twenty-two were from non-slaveholding States, and the
remaining ten members were either native Californians or old
settlers in that country. This prohibition against slavery, it
is said was inserted with entire unanimity. And it is this
circumstance, sir, the prohibition of slavery by that convention,
which has contributed to raise, I do not say wholly raised,

the dispute as to the propriety of the admission of California
into the Union under this constitution."

Mar. 11.   William H. Seward, of New York.
   Speech of William H. Seward, on the Admission of California,
   delivered in the Senate of the United States, March 11, 1850.
   Washington: Printed and For Sale by Buell & Blanchard,
   1850.
      46 pp. Printed wrapper.
   Same. Boston: Redding & Co., 1850.
      26 pp. Printed wrapper.
   California, Union, and Freedom. Speech of William H.
   Seward, on the Admission of California. Delivered in the
   Senate of the United States, March 11, 1850. (Printed by
   Buell & Blanchard.)
      16 pp. Caption title.
   Speech of the Hon. Wm. H. Seward, in the Senate of the
   United States, on the Admission of California. Delivered
   March 8, [sic] 1850.
      32 pp. Caption title.
   Includes speech of Cass, Mar. 13, pp. 19-32.
      Seward opened his speech with a few paragraphs of flowery
   oratory. "California, that comes from the clime where the
   west dies away into the rising east; California, that bounds at
   once the empire and the continent; California, the youthful
   queen of the Pacific, in her robes of freedom, gorgeously
   inlaid with gold — is doubly welcome."
      He then proceeded to answer the various objections to the
   admission of California, that had been voiced in the Senate,
   such as; California comes unceremoniously, without a preliminary consent of Congress; she has assigned her own boundaries, without the previous authority of Congress; she is too
   large; no census had been taken; and she comes under Executive influence.
      He predicted the Nation's population increase for every
   ten years for the next fifty, and in 1950 it would be 200,000,000
   and that the population on the Pacific Coast will far exceed
   what has heretofore occurred on the Atlantic Coast.

"California is already a State, a complete and fully appointed State. She can never again be less than that. She can never be a province or a colony; nor can she be made to shrink and shrivel into the proportions of a federal dependent territory . . . We shall never agree to admit California, unless we agree now. Nor will California abide delay. I do not say that she contemplates independence; but if she does not, it is because she does not anticipate rejection . . . I shall vote for the admission of California directly, without conditions, without qualifications, and without compromise."

Mar. 11. Orin Fowler.
Slavery in California and New Mexico. Speech of Mr. Orin Fowler, of Massachusetts, in the House of Representatives, March 11, 1850, in Committee of the Whole on the state of the Union, on the President's Message communicating the Constitution of California. (Buell & Blanchard, Printers.)
15 pp. Caption title.
"I am resolved to apply the [Wilmot] Proviso to that territory, not to injure any one's feelings, nor to wound any one's pride — but because it is constitutional and right, and, as I judge, eminently a prudent and practical measure."
This was a strong anti-slavery speech with no particular reference to California.
"The annexation was the cause of the war; and the result of the war is, we have Texas, New Mexico, and California. These acquisitions have not been the work of a day — Twenty-five years have been occupied upon it."

Mar. 11. Richard H. Stanton.
California and New Mexico. Speech of Hon. R. H. Stanton, of Kentucky, in the House of Representatives, March 11, 1850, In Committee of the Whole on the state of the Union, on the President's Message transmitting the Constitution of California. (Printed at the Congressional Globe Office.)
7 pp. Caption title.
This was a rabid pro-slavery argument, during which Stanton asked; if the institution of polygamy be allowed to

move into the territories, why not the institution of slavery?
"Without the shadow of authority, under any law or provision of the Constitution, the people of California have taken
the power into their own hands, and instituted all the machinery of State government... If the people have a right
to form a State government, without the authority of Congress,
they have a right to ask admission into the Union, or not, as
may suit their convenience or pleasure. There is no power
to compel a State to come into the Union, and if California
chooses, she may remain out indefinitely... Notwithunderstanding the wrong done to the South in excluding her from
California, notwithunderstanding the unprecedented and revolutionary character of her proceedings, by which the existing
state of things has been superinduced — I will waive all these,
and vote to admit her into the Union, with suitable boundaries, if northern men will meet me in a like spirit of concession."

Mar. 12.   **Hopkins L. Turney.**
Speech of Hon. H. L. Turney, of Tennessee, on the proposition to admit California as a State into the Union. Delivered
in the Senate of the United States, March 12, 1850.
Washington: Printed at the Congressional Globe Office.
1850.
12 pp.
Up to the last page and a half, this speech belied its title,
having nought to do with the admission of California, but
only with slavery; its constitutionality; its enemies; etc. When
at last Turney emerged from this to the subject of the title,
it was all negative.
"Now, Mr. President, a few more words, and I have done.
I refer to the question of the admission of California. I am
opposed to it. I have been unable to see any power on the
part of Congress to admit California with no organization
whatever — with no government — territorial or otherwise
— with no law beyond the law of the sword — the law of military authority... I say there is no state formed, whose constitution can be considered in any way. When we speak of
states, we speak of those which have a legal existence. Has

the State of California a legal existence? Where do we find it? It is wholly the work of a military commander, General Riley, calling a convention for the people of the territories ... The people did nothing in the matter for themselves. They were ordered to do what they did by a military chieftan."

Mar. 12.   Thomas B. Butler.

The Slave Question. Speech of Mr. Thos. B. Butler, of Connecticut, in the House of Representatives, March 12, 1850. In Committee of the Whole on the state of the Union, on the President's message transmitting the Constitution of California.

Printed in the Congressional Globe, no separate seen.

"The question before the committee, is upon the passage of the bill introduced by the gentleman from Wisconsin [Mr. Doty], providing for the admission of California, with the boundaries prescribed in her constitution. It is clearly certain that a very large majority of the House are in favor of the bill ... The frivolous objections relative to the organization of California as a State, I do not intend to argue."

Butler then plunged into an anti-slavery argument.

Mar. 12.   Willis A. Gorman.

Speech of Hon. W. A. Gorman, of Indiana, on the Admission of California. Delivered in the House of Representatives, Tuesday, March 12, 1850. Washington: Printed at the Congressional Globe Office. 1850.

8 pp.

The major portion of this speech was devoted to extolling the Democratic Party, of which Gorman was a member.

His plea was "admit California into the Union — settle the Texas boundary — organize the territories, leaving the people who are there in the fullest enjoyment of their inherent right to self-government — and abolish the slave trade in the District of Columbia."

He defended President Taylor in the California matter. Taylor being a Southerner and identified with the South by birth, education, pecuniary interests, and a slave-holder, would not be apt to try to influence the people of California through his agents, either civil or military, to form a state government with a clause in its constitution prohibiting slavery.

Mar. 13, 14.   Lewis Cass.

The Power of Congress over the Territories. Speech of Hon. Lewis Cass, of Michigan, in the Senate of the United States, March 13 and 14, 1850. On the Compromise Resolutions of Mr. Bell, of Tennessee, and the proposition to refer them to a Select Committee. (Printed at the Congressional Globe Office).

15 pp. Caption title.

Also included in one of the printings of Seward's March 11 speech. Pp. 19-32.

In reference to the resolutions, Cass said, "I am not prepared to say what my views will be upon the whole matter." However, he did indicate that he looked upon them with some favor, and declared; "I should vote for almost any proposition that had the appearance of bringing this Country into harmony on this perplexing question."

He criticized much that had been said on the floor of the Senate, at this and former sessions of Congress for the procrastination in the matter of establishing governments for the new territories. "Three sessions of Congress have intervened since these new territories came under the jurisdiction of the United States, and you have not legislated for them in a single instance, except to make provision for the collection of revenue at their ports . . . Without government they cannot exist; and you have provided no government for the people of California, and it is now contended, that they have no right to provide one for themselves."

Whether purposely used or not, Cass had the faculty of bringing an avalanche of interruptions and agitation upon himself, by weaving points and arguments of other Senators' speeches into his own. During this speech he was interrupted more than fifty times. In illustrating a point he repeated a story attributed to Benjamin Franklin which involved a jackass. At the end of the recitation, Butler said something

in a tone inaudible to the reporter, to which Cass replied;
"I go for the man, and not for the jackass." It could well be
that first name of "Jack" was applied to Cass at this stage of
his career.

Mar. 13, 14. Stephen A. Douglas.
Speech of Mr. Douglas, of Illinois, on the Territorial question.
Delivered in the Senate of the United States, March 13 and
14, 1850. Washington: Printed by John T. Towers. 1850.
> 31 pp.

The speech is opened with some severe criticisms of parts
of Webster's speech, then developed into a long-winded
argument against the extension of slavery into the new territories.

Mar. 13. David T. Disney.
Speech of Hon. David T. Disney, of Ohio, on the power of
Congress over the Territories. Delivered in the House of
Representatives, March 13, 1850. Washington: Printed at the
Congressional Globe Office. 1850.
> 14 pp.

This learned address includes but little directly upon the
California question, but clearly defines the constitutionally
limited power of Congress over the territories. "In the Declaration of Independence our fathers asserted, that all governments derive their just power from the consent of the governed
and if the principle be true, it is just as true in California as
it was in the old 13 colonies."

Mar. 14. Isaac E. Morse.
Speech of Hon. Isaac E. Morse, of Louisiana, on the President's
Message in relation to California. Delivered in the House of
Representatives, March 14, 1850. Washington: Printed at the
Congressional Globe Office. 1850.
> 8 pp.

The subject matter belies the title of this speech. Morse did
not commit himself to any stand on the California question,
but in the same tenor of his speech of February 24, 1849,

applies himself to the slavery question in general.

Mar. 14.   William Hebard.
Speech of Mr. Hebard, of Vermont, on the President's Message, communicating the Constitution of California. Delivered in the House of Representatives, U. S., in Committee of the Whole on the state of the Union, March 14, 1850. Washington: Gideon and Co., Printers. 1850.
   8 pp.
An anti-slavery discussion,
Hebard contended that Congress has the power to govern territories and restrict slavery therein, and to admit states into the Union without the necessity of any preliminary territorial government; also, that California should be admitted without any connection to a territorial government for New Mexico or any other issue.

Mar. 18, 19.   George E. Badger.
The Slavery Question. Speech of Mr. Badger, of North Carolina, in the Senate, March 18 and 19, 1850. The Senate having resumed the consideration of the Compromise Resolution offered by Mr. Clay, on the 25th of January.
   Printed in the Congressional Globe, no separate seen.
   At the end of his speech, Badger said that he will reluctantly vote for the admission of California for the harmony of the Union. On the territorial question he said nothing but that he felt that there was no likelihood of slavery going into the territories, and that the Wilmot proviso was entirely unnecessary for the government of these territories.

Mar. 18.   Christopher H. Williams.
Speech of Mr. C. H. Williams, of Tennessee, on the Admission of California, Delivered in the House of Representatives, March 18, 1850. (Towers, printer.)
   8 pp. Caption title.
   "Two years ago the Congress of the United States owed to California a territorial government; but the question of slavery stalked through this hall like Banquo's ghost, and

prevented Congressional action." On account of this Congressional procrastination, Williams justified the President's
action on the California matter, and declared that if California
was not admitted as a free state, but was remanded to territorial status, the Californians would not even then tolerate
slavery within their borders. He stood for the admission of
California, and was in agreement with Webster on the territorial governments for the residue without a slavery restriction. He unleashed considerable venom upon Stevens and
Seward, but he also was not in total accord with all of the
Southerners.

Mar. 18. Joseph Casey.
Speech of Mr. Casey, of Pennsylvania, on the President's
Message, communicating the Constitution of California. Delivered in the House of Representatives of the United States,
March 18, 1850. (Gideon & Co., Printers.)
    7 pp. Caption title.
    "I do not regard the institution of slavery as it exists in
our Southern States with that degree of horror which some
of my Northern brethern express; neither do I regard it as a
'great moral, political and religious blessing' with some
gentlemen of the South. I simply view it. in the language of
Thomas Jefferson, as 'a great moral and political evil.' "
    Casey viewed slavery as a local institution, existing only
by local laws, but with regard to the territories, they are
without local legislation, and only Congress has the power
to make laws for them. "Was there a single member of the
last Congress who, at the adjournment on the 4th of March,
1849, who did not believe and expect that the people of California would adopt the only alternative left them, of providing
for their own security and their own government? It was the
inevitable result of the most ungracious and unkind abandonment by this Government ... I am in favor of the admission
of California, with her present constitution and her present
boundaries, irrespective of all and every other question and
consideration."

Mar. 18.   Joshua R. Giddings.

Slavery in the Territories. Speech of Hon. J. R. Giddings, of
Ohio, in the House of Representatives, Monday, March 18,
1850, In Committee of the Whole on the state of the Union,
on the President's Message transmitting the Constitution of
California. (Printed and for sale by Buell & Blanchard, Sixth
Street, near Pensylvania Avenue, Price 50 cents per hundred.)
    8 pp. Caption title.

Giddings consumned his time on the floor in a tirade against
slavery and slave-holders. The reference to California was
but slight.

"I came here to enforce, to carry out the provisions of the
Constitution, not to compromise, nor surrender the rights
secured to us by that instrument."

Mar. 19.   John P. Hale.

Speech of Mr. Hale, of New Hampshire, on the Territorial
Question. Delivered in the Senate of the United States, March
19, 1850. (Printed and for sale by Buell & Blanchard.)
    16 pp. Caption title.

There was no direct mention of California, or any of the
other territories. Much was quoted from other speeches,
governmental acts, resolutions etc. going back as far as 1787
to support his arguments upon the non-extension of slavery.

Mar. 22.   William L. Dayton

The Territorial Question. Speech of Hon. W. L. Dayton, of
New Jersey, in the Senate of the United States, March 22,
1850. (Printed at the Congressional Globe Office.)
    16 pp. Caption title.

Dayton was contented to have California come into the
Union as a state under all circumstances with which she
applied for admission. He answerd some of the objections to
her admission; namely, that the admission under these circumstances would be an abandonment by this Government
of the sovereign power of legislation over territories; the
lack of a census; the extensive boundaries; and there was

no slave state ready to come into the Union to counterbalance
the free California.

"The North has been led along as by a string, blindfold,
for forty years, and now it has got in California a little start,
not by its wits, or by its wisdom, but by pure accident, and
the South says 'compromise or we secede' ".

For the sake of unity, Dayton felt that no prohibitive slavery
laws should be passed for New Mexico or Deseret, and was
convinced that nature herself will prohibit the extension of
slavery into these territories.

Mar. 25.   Robert M. T. Hunter

The Territorial Question. Speech of Hon. R. M. T. Hunter,
of Virginia, in the Senate of the United States, March 25, 1850.
(Printed at the Congressional Globe Office.)

15 pp. Caption title.

A pro-slavery speech, airing many Southern grievances
held against the North, but without a single reference to the
territorial question or California.

Mar. 25.   Samuel R. Thurston

Speech of Hon. S. R. Thurston, of Oregon, on the proposition
to admit California as a State into the Union. Delivered in
the House of Representatives, March 25, 1850. Washington:
Printed at the Congressional Globe Office. 1850.

21 pp.

Thurston was the first and only Representative in Congress
from the Pacific Coast at that time.

"The position which I intend to assume, Mr. Chairman, and
which I shall endeavor to make good by argument, is that
California should be admitted into the American Union as a
State on the terms she has asked." To make his points, he
quoted a resolution made in the Senate by Calhoun in 1847
to the effect that a people have the right to form a government
which is best suited to their needs, and if it be republican in
form, etc., Congress does not have the Constitutional power
to alter it, and quoted from the Constitution of California to
prove that it is republican in character.

He answered the objection to her long coast line by asserting that there are only two harbors that can be used to any extent (San Francisco and San Diego), so a coast line with so few harbors defeated the objection. The objection to her large size was answered by giving the square mileage of all of the Free States, including California as 509,340 square miles compared to 906,368 of the Slave States.

He gave a detailed account of the various steps that the people of California had made towards setting up their government, which movement would have gone forward just the same if General Riley had never issued his proclamation, or if the President's representative, King, had never seen California. He also read into his speech a letter he received from King, in which he disclaimed Presidential interference in the California matter, and dated his arrival at San Francisco the day after Riley's proclamation calling for a state government.

His speech was a very strong argument for the admission of California, not only for the arguments he developed, but in the mere fact that he was the sole Representative from a neighbor of California, and unusual in that he did not at any time digress from the subject.

Mar. 25. Daniel Breck.

Speech of Mr. Breck of Kentucky, on the Message of the President realating to California. Delivered in the House of Representatives of the United States, Monday, March 25, 1850.

16 pp. Caption title.

"It has been emphatically announced in this House and elsewhere, that if by any act of Congress, slavery shall be inhibited in these territories, or abolished in this District, the happening of either of these contingencies will induce immediate action in the South for its protection; or, in other words . . . will be followed by secession or revolution . . . I am decidedly opposed to both these measures."

Although Breck was born in the North, he represented a slave-holding State. He placed himself "in favor of a measure providing for the admission of California and the organization of territorial governments for the residue of California and New Mexico without the Wilmot proviso, leaving the question of slavery to be settled by the proper constitutional tribunal."

Mar. 25. Thomas L. Harris.
Admission of California. Speech of Hon. T. L. Harris, of Illinois, in the House of Representatives, March 25, 1850. In Committee of the Whole on the state of the Union, on the President's Message transmitting the Constitution of California. (Printed at the Congressional Globe Office.)
8 pp. Caption title.

In answer to some of the complaints emanating from Southern statesmen, here are a few interesting comparisons. The South claimed that more Federal money was expended in the North than in the South. Harris said that exclusive of naval and military installations, over a period of ten years, the amount expended in the North was 10 million dollars and in the South 9 million, but on a free white population basis, the North got $1.03 per person and the South $1.90. The postal receipts for 1833 were $1,109,000 and the expenditures $970,000 in the North, while in the South the receipts were $591,000 and the expenditures $962,000. For other years it was presumed that it differed but little.

For the Mexican war the South claimed that she had sent more soldiers into the field than the North. This was true, 47,600 men as against 24,700; when the months of service were computed, the North gave 309,400 months and the South 365,500 months. In the war of 1812, 215,000 men were drawn from the North and 256,000 from the South, but the North had 620,000 months of service to her credit and the South only 310,000 months.

"I am for the admission of California as a State into this Union — California as she is with her constitution and proposed boundaries."

Mar. 26, 27. Salmon P. Chase.
Union and Freedom, without Compromise. Speech of Mr. Chase, of Ohio, on Mr. Clay's Compromise Resolutions. In

Senate, March 26, 1850. (Printed and for sale by Buell &
Blanchard.)

16 pp. Caption title.

On the first day of the speech, Chase laboriously outlined
the history of slavery from its beginning in 1620 to the time
of his speech. He included the effect of various ordinances
and provisos aimed at it, earlier statesmen's attitude towards
it and many paragraphs from the American archives, Madison
letters, Elliot debates and others, together with some statistical
data.

He went into the matter of Clay's compromise on the
second day, of which he was not particularly in favor. "The
first proposition of the Senator from Kentucky relates to the
admission of California. It is not now a matter of dispute
whether California shall or shall not be admitted into the
Union. That question is settled. No one doubts that California
is to come in, with the boundaries which she claims and with
the Constitution she has adopted. I concur cordially in this
decision. As a Western man, I should have preferred the
erection of two States rather than one out of the Territory
acquired from Mexico on the Pacific; and I wish also, in
common with many of the most intelligent citizens of California, that her eastern boundary had been restricted to the
range of the Sierra Nevada. Under existing circumstances,
however, I desire to see California come in as she is, without
restriction and without delay."

Mar. 27, Apr. 3.   Roger S. Baldwin.

Speech of Hon. R. S. Baldwin, of Connecticut, in favor of the
Admission of California into the Union, and on the Territorial Bills, and the Bill in relation to Fugitive Slaves, in
connection with Mr. Bell's Compromise Resolutions. Delivered
in the Senate of the United States, March 27 and April 3,
1850. Washington: Printed at the Congressional Globe Office.
1850.

20 pp.

Baldwin was not in favor of Bell's compromise, or any
other bill that might be attached to the California bill.

"The declaration of independence, too, was not an act
competent to the colonial legislatures; it was an act of original
inherent sovereignty by the people themselves, in whose name
they undertook to act and to declare these United States to
be one people. But if the act of California were to be regarded
even as a revolutionary measure, and not merely an irregular
exercise of their right under the [Mexican] treaty, by a people
desirous of coming into the Union, and enjoying the rights
and protection stipulated by treaty, we should all be ready
to admit that it is less obnoxious to censure than a revolutionary act by an old State with a view to disunion and all the
disastrous consequences that would follow."

Mar. 27.   George Ashmun.
Slavery Question. Speech of Mr. G. Ashmun, of Massachusetts,
in the House of Representatives, March 27, 1850. The House
being in Committee of the Whole on the state of the Union,
on the President's message communicating the Constitution
of California.
    Printed in the Congressional Globe, no separate seen.
    "I desire to set out at the start with the declaration that I
shall sustain the bill for the admission of California as a state,
which is now before us, unembarrassed by, and disconnected
from, all other propositions."
    In Ashmun's opinion the present slavery agitation com-
menced with the annexation of Texas. "It was that stupendous
scheme for the extension of slavery — conceived in iniquity
and brought forth in sin, which fully aroused the slumbering
anti-slavery feelings of the Northern people." Before that,
there were abolition societies, which had little connection with
political questions, but since the annexation of Texas, with
the possibility of four additional slave states that might be
carved out of her, the activities of these societies increased
to the point of meddling with slavery as it existed within the
states. This not only tended to check the progress of emancipation sentiment and movement, particularly in Virginia and
Kentucky, but contributed to fasten more tightly the chains
of slaves in all of the slave states.

Mar. 27, 28. Thomas H. Averett.

Speech of Hon. T. H. Averett, of Virginia, on the Proposition to Admit California as a State into the Union. Delivered in the House of Representatives, March 27, 1850 Washington: Printed at the Congressional Globe Office. 1850.

12 pp.

The speech was naturally pro-slavery in character, and advocated the extension of slavery into California.

"The President has declared Mexican law in force; under it there is worse bondage than exists anywhere else on this continent. The peonage system makes the debtor the slave of his creditor; the miserable peons of Mexico serve in more abject slavery, than do our black slaves."

"The President has incited and urged the adventurers, mixed breeds, and alien sojourners in California, to form for themselves a State government and assume jurisdiction over the country, and now urges us to sanction that assumption." "Look to the debates in the California Convention, and you will see the incipient symptoms of disaffection to this Government already." Averett assumed that the "adventurers, mixed breeds, and alien adventurers" will not protect indivdual property rights or Government interests.

Mar. 28. Joseph R. Chandler.

Speech of Mr. J. R. Chandler, of Penn., on the Admission of California: Delivered in the House of Representatives of the United States, March 28, 1850. Washington: Gideon & Co., printers. 1850.

15 pp.

"The peace with Mexico secured to these United States the possession of a vast territory, which brought with it the laws of sovereignty for which it had been received — laws which must, by the customs of nations, and the decisions of the United States Court, continue to be operative until new laws and ordinances shall be extended over them. The people of the United States who floocked to California with the first intimation of the discovery of gold were not men to approve of the laws of Mexico; and indeed there were very

few to make known those laws there, and fewer to enforce
them. Yet these people, emigrants from the various States,
were imbued with a reverence for laws, and had a full
knowledge of the propriety of some machinery of government,
by which laws could be enacted, or at least respectably ad-
ministered. As in the newly settled portion of California, the
Mexican laws were little known, they sought to take measures
to secure for themselves the proper operation of the laws of
the United States. But while they deliberated, the Congress
of the Union discussed, debated, hesitated, and then failed,
to give them what they needed . . . They have proceeded as
other people have proceeded; they have delibrately, orderly,
and with all republican forms, prepared and adopted a constitution for a sovereign state; . . . Admit California with such
institutions as she desires, and wait a year. . . . and see what
New Mexico will ask."

Apr. 3. Humphrey Marshall.
California and New Mexico. Speech of Hon. H. Marshall, of
Kentucky, in the House of Representatives, April 3, 1850. In
Committee of the Whole on the state of the Union, on the
President's Message transmitting the Constitution of Califor-
nia. (Printed at the Congressional Globe Office.)
  8 pp. Caption title.
  "I am no propagandist of slavery because I consider it a
moral, social, and political blessing. I heartily wish it had
never existed on the continent; but as a system of labor, one
half of the States have become accustomed to it — ."
  He suggested the extension of the Missouri compromise line,
and was willing that it be diverted south upon reaching the
California boundary, thus excluding slaves from California.
He cared nothing for the equilibrium of slave and free states,
and was willing that California be admitted under her submitted constitution: "Dressed in her robes of freedom,
gorgeously inlaid with gold, the young Queen of the Pacific."

Apr. 3. William A. Richardson.
Speech of Hon. W. A. Richardson, of Illinois, on the admission

of California. Delivered in the House of Representatives, April 3, 1850. Washington: Printed at the Congressional Globe Office. 1850.

7 pp.

Richardson had the conviction that slavery would not thrive in any of the new territories, and that these territories will be peopled by pioneers, who will not tolerate the competition of slavery, and will eventually set up free state governments long before slave-holders find it agreeable to move there.

"Admit California as a state into the Union with the boundaries as the people have fixed them; pass a bill for a territorial goverment for the residue of the country, saying not one word about slavery; leave the people who go, when they shall apply admission, to determine for themselves what their institutions shall be."

Apr. 4. Elbridge G. Spaulding.

President's Plan. Speech of Hon. E. G. Spaulding, of New York, in favor of Gen. Taylor's Plan for admitting California and New Mexico, and contrasting the Chicago Convention with the proposed Nashville Convention. Delivered in the House of Representatives of the United States, April 4, 1850. (Gideon & Co., Print.)

16 pp. Caption title.

Referring to the President's message, recommending the admission of California, Spaulding said; "I do not hesitate to declare, that I am in favor of standing by the President in what I conceive to be a wise and patriotic recommendation. I am for admitting California as she is, with her present constitution and boundaries, disconnected from all other subjects."

He made a point of the fact that the Executive Department, under President Polk, through military and naval appointees to the de facto governments in the territories, continued with the laws of Mexico. This precluded slavery so long as this government functioned.

The President's message of January 21, 1850 to the House is included in the printing of this speech.

Apr. 4.   James S. Green.
California and New Mexico. Speech of Hon. James S. Green, of Missouri, in the House of Representatives, April 4, 1850. In Committee of the Whole on the state of the Union, on the President's Message transmitting the Constitution of California. (Printed at the Congressional Globe Office.)
8 pp. Caption title.

A proposition was submitted by Green by which all of the territory acquired from Mexico would be divided into free soil and slave soil by the extension of the Missouri compromise line to the Pacific Ocean. This pro-slavery speech was in support of the proposition.

According to him, at the time the convention assembled in California to form a state government, the members were acquainted with the high anti-slavery feeling of the majority in Congress, so in order to promote the admission of the State they inserted a clause in their constitution prohibiting slavery. When the question of slavery was pending before the convention, it was not allowed to be voted upon by the people as a separate article, but was embodied in the constitition and thus handed to the voters to insure its passing. This, in his estimation, formed an objection to admission, together with the so-called Executive interference and "unreasonable" boundary claims.

Apr. 5.   James Shields.
Speech of Mr. Shields, of Illinois, on the Territorial Question. Delivered in the Senate of the United States, April 5, 1850. Washington: Printed by Jno. T. Towers. 1850.
16 pp.

"I am in favor of the admission of California into the Union as a State, here there is no room for compromise. . . . Whether California is a State or a Territory, whether it has any government or no government, no Southern slave owner will ever venture to carry his slaves into that country . . . The people of California are working out a great social problem — a problem that has never been worked out successfully any where else: and that is, to make labor — hard labor, dignified

and respectable ... the high-spirited sons of Southern gentlemen, would be the first to resist and resent such an experi-
ment ... In California at this moment, there are one hundred
and fifty thousand men; not old men, women and children, but
young, active, daring adventurous men — the flower of the
youth of our country — men such as never settled a new
country before ... the South and the North, and the whole
country united can never force slavery on them."

Apr. 8.   Thomas H. Benton.
The Admission of California. Speech of Hon. T. H. Benton,
of Missouri, in the Senate of the United States, April 8, 1850.
On the Compromise Resolutions of Mr. Bell, of Tennessee,
and the proposition to refer them to a Select Committee.
8 pp. Caption title.
"I ask for California a separate consideration, and object
to mixing her up with any, much more with the whole of the
angry and distracting subjects of difference which have grown
up out of slavery in the United States.
What are these subjects? They are:
1.   The creation of Territorial Governments in New Mexico, and in the remaining part of California.
2.   The creation of a new State in Texas, reduction of her
boundaries, settlement of her dispute with New Mexico, and
cession of her surplus territory to the United States.
3.   Recapture of fugitive slaves.
4.   Suppression of the slave trade in the District of Columbia.
5.   Abolition of slavery in the District of Columbia.
6.   Abolition of slavery in the forts, arsenals, navy-yards,
and dock yards of the United States.
7.   Abolition of the slave trade between the States.
8.   Abolition of slavery within the States."
Each one of these points was then expanded to sustain his
objection to any of them being appended to the California
question.
He took up the various objections that had been offered to
the admission of California.

"1. That no act of Congress has been passed to authorize the people of California to form a state constitution. The fact is admitted, but its consequence is denied. Congress has the full power over the admission of new States, and may dispense with all preliminary forms, when it pleases, and come direct to the question of admission . . .

2. Aliens voting at the election of members of the convention. The fact may be so — probably was so . . . The framers of the Texan constitution were all aliens; and yet did not prevent her admission . . .

3. Insufficient number — not people enough — . . . About ten or twelve thousand; for that is the number of men which the usually required population of a new State would give. One man to six souls is the usual proportion . . . Her [California's] man population was computed at about one hundred thousand when her constitution was formed . . .

4. . . . The State is said to be too large — that she cut and carved too largely for herself. That objection comes with an ill grace from us, who took in Texas, five years ago, three times as large as California . . .

5. It is objected that President Taylor interfered to induce the people of California to make this State government . . . President Taylor did not interfere."

Apr. 8. Daniel Wallace.
The Slavery Question. Speech of Hon. Daniel Wallace, of South Carolina, in the House of Representatives, April 8, 1850, In Committee of the Whole on the state of the Union, on the President's Message communicating the Constitution of California. (Printed at the Congressional Globe Office.)
7 pp. Caption title.
After tracing the various steps by which the South with its institution of slavery has been circumvented from expansion, Wallace approached the subject of California. His argument was, that all of the states, excepting the original thirteen, had not come into the Union as states without some previous territorial preparation, and that all of the territories from which these later states developed were ceded either by the original

thirteen states, or by a foreign power to the Federal Government. "By what authority, then, have the congregation of adventurers, from all nations calling themselves the people of California, entered upon these lands, and appropriated to themselves the mineral wealth they contain, in derogation of the rights of the United States? By what authority have these trespassers upon public property met in convention, formed what they call a state constitution, and sent their Senators and Representatives here, to ask admission into the Union? . . . The fact is overlooked, that there is a period, during which the inhabitants of a territory do not possess the attributes of sovereignty . . . Why not wait until the anarchy which prevails there now, subsides into organic order, and their pretentions to dignity and rights of an independent State be founded upon reasonable grounds? The answer to all these questions is plain. The movement is that of the abolition party."

Apr. 8. James L. Johnson.
Speech of Mr. J. L. Johnson, of Kentucky, on the Admission of California: Delivered in the House of Representatives of the United States, April 8, 1850. (Gideon & Co., Print.)
15 pp. Caption title.
Johnson objected to the immediate admission of California on the grounds that no census had been taken, and that her boundaries had not yet been approved. However, he declared that he would vote for her admission bill if it was offered with a bill for establishing a territorial government for the residue of territory without the Wilmot proviso.

Apr. 9. Moses B. Corwin.
Speech of Hon. Moses B. Corwin, of Ohio, on the proposition to Admit California as a State into the Union. Delivered in the House of Representatives, April 9, 1850. Washington: Printed at the Congressional Globe Office. 1850.
7 pp.
Corwin was rigidly opposed to any extension of slavery, and stated that there is more uncultivated land now existing

in the Southern States than can be made use of in the next
ten generations.

He was not favorably inclined towards any compromise
being tacked on the California bill.

Apr. 9. Isham G. Harris.

Admission of California. Speech of Hon. I. G. Harris, of
Tennessee, in the House of Representatives, April 9, 1850.
In Committee of the Whole on the state of the Union, on the
President's Message transmitting the Constitution of Cali-
fornia. (Printed at the Congressional Globe Office.)

7 pp. Caption title.

The main point of argument in this speech was that Congress
has not the power to restrict slavery. Harris said; "give territorial governments to Deseret and New Mexico, without any
restriction upon the subject of slavery — admit California;
pass some law rendering effective that provision of the Constitution which requires the delivering up of fugitive slaves es-
caping into free States."

Apr. 10. Thomas Ross.

Speech of Hon. Thos. Ross, of Pennsylvania, on the Admission
of California. Delivered in the House of Representatives, April
10, 1850. Washington: Printed at the Congressional Globe
Office. 1850.

12 pp.

Ross did not favor the admission of California. He feared
her size; her harbors, with the advantage of far eastern trade;
her immense mineral wealth will induce a dense population,
even though "I am aware that a great part of her soil is barren
and will be unproductive," all of which will lead to a western
empire, which might be inclined to establish its independence,
or have a preponderance of national representation. "The
smaller we make the States on the Pacific, the greater will be
our security against secession."

"But there are other objections to the admission of California,
beside the extent of her territory. Has she served the pro-
bationary period which has heretofore been required of all

our territories? Has her population in one year become sufficiently indoctrinated in republican principles? ... When I speak of population, I do not mean gold-seekers and other adventurers who have gone there for a temporary object; but what is the number of her resident population? ... The whole number of votes polled was only about 12,800, and that too, without any regard to residence or any other qualification of the voter." That number does not entitle her to even one representative in Congress.

Apr. 10.   William Duer.

The Territorial Question. Speech of Hon. William Duer, of New York, in the House of Representatives, April 10, 1850. In Committee of the Whole on the state of the Union, on the President's Message communicating the Constitution of California. (Printed at the Congressional Globe Office.)

8 pp. Caption title.

There was little reference to California in this speech. Duer voted against the Wilmot proviso being applied to the proposed territorial governments for the territories not included within the boundaries of California, along with two other Northern Representatives. He was of the opinion that the territories themselves should be given the right to include or exclude slavery in their ultimate state constitutions. "There is no doubt of the power of a State to prohibit slavery, while we know that the power of Congress is seriously disputed."

Apr. 18.   Andrew Ewing.

Speech of Mr. Andrew Ewing, of Tennessee, on the Admission of California. Delivered in the House of Representatives, April 18, 1850. Washington: Printed by John T. Towers. 1850.

15 pp.

Ewing made note of the fact that the "chaos of strife and confusion has measurably cleared away," in the House.

At this time there were two plans offered: one that California be admitted with no further action as to the other territories until they were ready for statehood; the other that California be admitted and that territorial governments be created for Utah and New Mexico, without a slavery restriction, and an acknowledgement of the boundaries of Texas. Ewing rejected the first plan, and about the other said; "there is no prospect that she [California] will ever change her attitude in regard to slavery. If we remand her back to a territorial condition, the prospect is, that she might renounce our allegiance and that we should have to imbrue our hands in the blood of our brethern before the stars and stripes would again float triumphant on the shores of the Pacific . . . I am therefore for the admission of California."

Apr. 18.   William J. Alston.
The Slavery Question. Speech of Hon. Wm. J. Alston, of Alabama, in the House of Representatives, April 18, 1850. In Committee of the Whole on the state of the Union, on the President's Message transmitting the Constitution of California. (Printed at the Congressional Globe Office.)
    8 pp. Caption title.
    A pro-slavery speech, citing and quoting the Bible to make his points. There was no mention of California, or other territories in the entire speech.

Apr. 19.   Chauncey F. Cleveland.
The California Question. Speech of Hon. Chauncey F. Cleveland, of Connecticut, in the House of Representatives, April 19, 1850. In Committee of the Whole on the state of the Union, on the President's Message transmitting the Constitution of California. (Printed at the Congressional Globe Office.)
    8 pp. Caption title.
    Cleveland was an outspoken, uncompromising abolitionist. He took an unwavering stand against slavery and the extension of slavery into any of the territories, and condemned all those who did not. "As one of the soldiers in this battle, I protest against a base surrender of the rights of freedom. I do it, sir, for my constituents, my State, myself — for seventeen millions of human beings who have no interest in the extension of slavery, and for three million of beings fashioned

in the image of their Creator, who are held in cruel, crushing
bondage."

Apr. 22. Thomas H. Benton.

California debate. Mr. Benton's Anti-tack Speech, or speech
against tacking anything to the California State admission
bill, on his motion to instruct the Committee of Thirteen to
that effect. Delivered in the Senate of the United States,
Monday, April 22, 1850. Washington: Printed at the Congressional Globe Office. 1850.

8 pp.

This adds nothing on the California question that was not
covered by Benton's speech of April 8. It is almost entirely
on parliamentary procedure.

Apr. 23. Charles S. Morehead.

Speech of Mr. Morehead, of Kentucky, on the Admission of
California, and the Question of Slavery. Delivered in the
House of Representatives of the United States, April 23, 1850.
Washington: Printed by Gideon & Co., 1850.

15 pp.

The tenor of this speech is much the same as his speech
of February 24, 1849.

He called the whole proceedings of California presenting
a constitution and asking admission extremely irregular, but
said; "I have made up my mind to vote for her admission,
provided that admission can be made the basis of an amicable
and harmonious settlement of the distracting questions which
are convulsing the country." The latter part of this declaration
is clarified in several following paragraphs, which boil down
to the fact that he wanted territorial governments set up for
the residue without slavery restrictions.

Apr. 23. Lucius B. Peck.

Slavery in the Territories. Speech of Hon. Lucius B. Peck,
of Vermont, in the House of Representatives, April 23, 1850,
In Committee of the Whole on the state of the Union, on the
President's Message transmitting the Constitution of Cali-

fornia. (Printed at the Congressional Globe Office.)
8 pp. Caption title.

About one-half of this speech was directly upon the California question, clearly put, without oratorical digressions.

He refuted three of the main objections to the admission of
California, i.e., that Congress had not authorized the people
to form a state government; that the constitution was drawn
by adventurers; and that her boundaries are too extensive.

The balance of the speech referred to establishing territorial
governments for the residual territory. "I go for establishing
territorial governments, with the Ordinance of 1787 ingrafted
thereon." This would, of course, prohibit slavery there.

May 3. David Wilmot.

Slavery in the Territories. Speech of Hon. D. Wilmot, of
Pennsylvania, in the House of Representatives. May 3, 1850,
In Committee of the Whole on the state of the Union, on the
President's Message transmitting the Constitution of Cali-
fornia. (Printed at the Congressional Globe Office.)
8 pp. Caption title.

As Wilmot gave his name to the proviso, which if applied
to any of the territories would exclude slavery therefrom, he
could only argue against the extension of it. He claimed that
it would eventually go there if it was not curbed by law. He
condemned the southern aristocracy and their Congressmen
for the agitation and unrest now engulfing the Country.

The references to the admission of California were but
slight, and then only in connection with a possible accompany-
ing compromise bill for effecting governments for the territories.

May 8. Robert C. Winthrop.

Admission of California. Speech of the Hon. R. C. Winthrop,
of Mass., on the President's Message, transmitting the Constitution of California: Delivered in Committee of the Whole in
the House of Representatives of the United States, May 8,
1850. Washington: Gideon & Co., Printers. 1850.
28 pp.

Although egotistical in parts, but unlike the speech of
February 21st in character, this speech brought forth many
substantial arguments.

The political prospects of all the territories from Texas to
the Canadian border were discussed. On the admission of
California question, Winthrop took the stand that it should
be presented alone, with no bills or compromises appended.

"Today, it [California] presents itself to us an established
Commonwealth ... Shall it be remanded to its colonial condition? Shall we attempt to crowd this full-grown man into
the cradle of infancy? ... Is it said that she has not population
enough? The best accounts which we can obtain estimate her
population at more than a hundred thousand souls; and these,
be it remembered are nearly all full-grown persons, and the
vast majority of them are men, and voters ... Is it said that
her boundaries are too extensive? You did not find fault with
Texas ... Do you complain of the length of her sea-coast?
You did not find fault with Florida ... Is it said that her
constitution has been cooked? ... we have a Southern President, and a majority of Southern men in the Cabinet; and
they sent a Southern agent . . . to bear their dispatches and
communicate their views to the California settlers. Is it said
that these settlers are a wild, reckless, floating population,
bent only on digging gold, and unworthy to be trusted in
establishing a government? Sir, I do not believe a better class
of emigrants was ever found flocking in such numbers to any
new settlement on the face of the earth ... Is it said, finally,
Mr. Chairman, as a ground for rejecting California, that she
has prohibited slavery in her constitution? ... Even those
who would willingly have it otherwise, must be glad in their
own hearts, whether they confess it or not, that she has
settled that question for herself."

May 8. James L. Orr.
The Slavery Question. Speech of Hon. J. L. Orr, of South
Carolina, in the House of Representatives, May 8, 1850, in
Committee of the Whole on the state of the Union, on the
President's Message transmitting the Constitution of Califor-

nia. (Printed at the Congressional Globe Office.)

7 pp. Caption title.

Orr objected to the admission of California on the grounds that no census had been taken to ascertain the number of representatives to be sent to Congress; a convention to frame a constitution was called, not by Congress, but by a military officer. "After the convention was elected, it assembled, and by a vote for which it had no authority, not even from the military dictator, it increased the number of delegates from thirty-seven to seventy-nine, and allowed the additional number, without referring it to the people, to take their seats, they being the defeated candidates at the election."

"Who are the people of California? A world in minature [sic] — the four quarters of the globe are represented there. No naturalization laws having been passed, there was no legal impediment to their exercising the right of suffrage. The whole proceeding — not having the consent of Congress, the rightful legislature of the territory — was illegal and revolutionary."

May 13. Henry Clay.

Speech of Henry Clay, of Kentucky, on the report of the Committee of Thirteen. Delivered in the Senate of the United States, May 13, 1850. (Towers, printer.)

16 pp. Caption title.

Clay pointed out to some of the objectors that California has a sufficient population to entitle her to two Representatives. The ratio was fixed at 70,680 by law, but also more than half again or a total of 106,021 entitles any state to two Representatives.

On the first of January of 1849, California had a population of 26,000, of which 8,000 were Americans, 13,000 Californians and 5,000 foreigners. A year later the population had increased to 107,069 "partly conjectural it is true," and March 27, 1850, the population was 124,026, to which must be added 14,240 officers and seamen who had deserted their ships.

"I think, then, Mr. President, that with respect to the population of California, with respect to the limits of California, and with respect to the circumstances under which she presents herself to Congress for admission as a State into the Union, all are favorable to grant her what she solicits." The speech was in further support of his compromise.

May 13. John H. Savage.

The California Question. Speech of Mr. John H. Savage, of Tennessee, in the House of Representatives, May 13, 1850. Printed in the Congressional Globe, no separate seen.

It seems obvious that Savage endeavored to live up to the meaning of his name. His attack upon the President was no less than savage. If it was not for the interference of the Executive, "California would now be under the protection of Congress, and not the pupil King [the President's agent in California] . . . I consider the territorial policy of the present Executive a lawless interference with the rights of the people there, and the action of Congress here.

"California became the joint property of the people of this Republic, upon which each of its proprietors might lawfully enter with his peculiarity. A joint title in all laws gives the right to a joint possession and enjoyment, independent of person, habits, or occupation. The slaveholder must come with his slave, and the northern man with his manufacturers: . . . To admit California as she is now, would, in my opinion, be to do a thing wrong itself . . . I object to her boundary, and the mode of her coming, . . . yet I may, perhaps, vote for her admission, provided governments for the territories are formed at the same time, neither enacting or abolishing slavery therein, but submitting that question to God and the people who may settle them. I know of no higher tribunals than these—Saint Seward and certain other Saints on this floor to the contrary notwithunderstanding."

May 13. Charles E. Clarke.

Speech of Hon. Chas. E. Clarke, of New York, on the Admission of California. Delivered in the House of Representatives, May 13, 1850. Washington: Printed at the Congressional Globe Office. 1850.

16 pp.

An anti-slavery speech with very little said on the California
question. He had a strong central government conviction,
stating; "In the territories lately acquired, the United States
not only has absolute sovereignty, but is to a great extent
the owner of the soil; and every squatter, every man who
has cut a tree or dug an ounce of gold, is legally responsible
to the owner of the soil." However he stated; "I am particularly glad that California is here with her constitution claiming
rights that are secured to her by treaty, and am at all times
ready to welcome her to our Union."

May 14. George W. Julian.
Speech of Hon. George W. Julian, of Indiana, on the Slavery
Question, delivered in the House of Representatives, May 14,
1850. Washington: Printed at the Congressional Globe Office.
1850.
15 pp.
This was an anti-slavery speech with but one slight reference to California. It was, of course, sparked by the months
of agitation over the California and territorial questions.
Julian pointed out that in 1803 fifteen million dollars were
given for the Louisiana territory, out of which was carved the
Slave States of Louisiana, Arkansas and Missouri; in 1819
five millions were spent for Florida, another slave state, and
in 1845 Texas was annexed bringing with it the possibility
that it might be dismembered into four or five more slave
states, and altogether nine slave states had been added to
the Union since its formation.
"Some thirty years ago the States of Kentucky, Tennessee,
Alabama and Missouri were more or less incumbered with an
Indian population. The white man and his slave were shut
out from large regions of those States by the barriers of the
red man ... All these regions are now redeemed from the
Indian, ... done by the help of northern votes."

May 14. James Meacham.
The California Question. Speech of Hon. James Meacham,
of Vermont, in the House of Representatives, May 14, 1850,

In Committee of the Whole on the state of the Union, on Mr. McClernand's Bill relating to California. (Printed at the Congressional Globe Office.)

8 pp. Caption title.

McClernand's bill called for: 1. The admission of California: 2. Territorial goverment for Utah: 3. Territorial government for the residue of the acquisition from Mexico, called New Mexico: 4. Settlement of the Texas — New Mexico boundary.

Meacham said much in general, but little in particular upon the subject.

"But when you have given up all controversy about California, why link it with others, many of them old and offensive, about which there is dispute? Why bind the carcass to the living man? I have a right to put myself and my constituents on record in her favor."

May 15, 16 and 20. Henry S. Foote.

California, Territorial Governments. &c. Remarks of Hon. Mr. Foote, of Mississippi, on the Plan of adjusting the questions growing out of Slavery, reported from the special committee of the Senate. Delivered in the Senate, May 15, 16, and 20, 1850.

16 pp. Caption title.

After the death of Calhoun it would appear that Foote assumed the leadership of the Southern side of the Senate, at least he got into most every debate, had more to say, and seemed to have had more ideas for the solution of the California and territorial questions. He was an able speaker, and although imbued with the institution of slavery, many of his ideas were quite sound, from that point of view.

Most of these remarks were leveled at Yulee of Florida and Clemens of Alabama, berating their attitude towards the territorial question involving the status of the Mexican abolition of slavery.

He was adamant about there being some offset to the admission of California favoring the South. One of his earlier schemes, mentioned here, was to erect a new state from the eastern part of Texas, but was now content to f a v o r the compromise, for which he claimed to have been laboring, since the beginning of the session.

May 16 and 20. Jeremiah Clemens.

California, Territorial Governments, &c. Speech of Hon. J. Clemens, of Alabama, in the Senate of the United States, May 16 and 20, 1850. On the Bill to admit California as a State into the Union, to establish Territorial Governments for Utah and New Mexico, and making proposals to Texas for the establishment of her western boundary.

8 pp. Caption title.

The first day of this speech, using half of the allotted hour, might well be described as the bickerings of Southern Senators upon a proviso that they intended to attach to the California bill, which provided that no laws be passed restricting any United States citizen from going into any of these territories with all of his property.

The second day was more on the same subject, but by quoting from various other speeches, he avoided interruptions.

May 21. Pierre Soulé.

The Compromise Question. Speech of Mr. Soulé, of Louisiana, in the Senate, May 21, 1850.

Printed in the Congressional Globe, no separate seen.

Soulé enumerated what he called the question of controversy between the North and the South.

1. South to have equal share in the territories acquired from Mexico.

2. South's denial of the right of Congress to interfere with slavery in the District of Columbia, or obstruct the slave trade between states.

3. To have the provisions of the Constitution directing the delivery of fugitive slaves effectively enforced.

4. The boundary rights of Texas.

He argued against all of the measures of the Clay compromise, excepting the first, the admission of California, to which he was favorable as a separate bill.

On the question of slavery in the territories, he had considerable to say. To those who maintain that the Mexican laws prohibiting slavery still obtain, he asked, if the Mexican tariff laws with all the penalties and confiscations, should not be revived also. Mexican laws treat Americans as foreigners; while they are in force, Americans would not have the right to hold office, vote, or be officers in the militia. The same laws prohibit African slavery, but tolerate peonage, "so the Free-Soilers will have to make their choice between black slavery and white slavery."

May 21. Henry Clay.
The Compromise Bill. Speech of Mr. Clay, of Kentucky, in the Senate, May 21, 1850.
Printed in the Congressional Globe, no separate seen.
Once again Clay spoke for his compromise bill as being the only relief from the embarrassing agitation initiated by the California question.
"If you do not pass this measure, there is a possibility that the California bill will not pass. I have no doubt myself but that there are large majorities in both Houses of Congress in favor of the admission of California into the Union; but from causes upon which I shall not dwell . . . I am afraid that that bill never will pass the two Houses as a measure by itself." He was not right about this.

May 21. Daniel P. King.
The California Question and the Ordinance of '87. Speech of Hon. D. P. King of Massachusetts, in the House of Representatives, May 21, 1850. In Committee of the Whole on the state of the Union, on the President's Message transmitting the Constitution of California. (Printed at the Congressional Globe Office.)
8 pp. Caption title.
"I go for the admission of California, not for the sake of her golden sands, but for the sake of the right — a treasure more valuable than all the gold and silver and precious stones of which avarice in her wildest vagaries has ever dreamed.

I shall vote for the admission of California with its constitution prohibiting slavery, without qualification, without restriction, without limitation, and without delay."

May 21. Thomas S. Haymond.
Speech of Hon. T. S. Haymond, of Virginia, on the Admission of California. Delivered in the House of Representatives, May 21, 1850. Washington: Printed at the Congressional Globe Office. 1850.
8 pp.

Haymond took exception to his Southern colleagues and stood for the admission of California in which he saw no "serious evil ... If any difficulty shall arise, it will grow out of the effort to establish territorial governments for New Mexico and Utah."

He also took exception to his colleagues who charged that the President usurped legislative power to direct the formation of the State of California through an agent, whereas the President only suggested to the people of California the propriety of forming a state government. He was the first Southerner to approve the President's action from the floor of the House.

May 21. Elbridge Gerry.
The Slavery Question. Speech of Mr. E. Grrry [sic], of Maine, in the House of Representatives, Tuesday, May 21, 1850. In Committee of the Whole on the state of the Union, on the President's message transmitting the constitution of California.

Printed in the Congressional Globe, no separate seen.

Gerry gave little time to discussing the California and territorial questions, only to mention that he favored the admission of California and the organization of the territories of New Mexico and Utah, with a provision interdicting slavery.

The speech was primarily an anti-slavery discussion, including some uncomplimentary remarks aimed at President Taylor, even to calling him "Janus-faced."

May 22. Solomon W. Downs.

The Compromise Bill. Speech of Mr. Downs, of Louisiana, in the Senate, May 22, 1850.

Printed in the Congressional Globe, no separate seen.

Downs was favorable toward the compromise, not on every point, but believed it was the best that the South could obtain.

He accepted the fact of California's self determination, but was not particularly pleased with her size, which took from the Mexican acquisition about a third or a fourth of the most valuable part of the whole. He consoled himself with the presumption that the residue, particularly New Mexico, might be more valuable than it was thought to be.

"What reason have we to believe that we shall gain anything in the South by defeating this compromise? . . . We have at no time so favorable a compromise offered us as this."

May 24. Pierre Soulé.

The Compromise Bill. Speech of P. Soulé, of Louisiana, in the Senate of the United States, May 24, 1850.

Printed in the Congressional Globe, no separate seen.

Soulé skipped over the first resolution of the compromise, which had to do with California; had a few words to say on the second (territorial governments for Utah and New Mexico); but had much to say on the sixth (slave trade in the District of Columbia). After about one-third of the speech was spoken, the complexion of the attitude in the Senate changed, and from there on the speech became a general debate.

May 27. James M. Mason.

The Compromise Bill. Speech of Mr. Mason, of Virginia, in the Senate, May 27, 1850.

Printed in the Congressional Globe, no separate seen.

Mason favored the extension of the Missouri compromise line to the Pacific.

His argument being that it would cut off four and one-half degrees of latitude from the proposed State of California and open all of that portion south to slavery.

He objected to that part of the compromise bill which had
to do with the Texas — New Mexico boundary, by which
Texas would be shorn of much territory that would, as part
of Texas, definitely tolerate slavery, but if awarded to New
Mexico there was some doubt as to slave status.

May 27. James H. Thomas.

Admission of California. Speech of Hon. J. H. Thomas, of
Tennessee, in the House of Representatives, May 27, 1850,
In Committee of the Whole on the state of the Union, on the
President's Message transmitting the Constitution of Cali-
fornia.

8 pp. Caption title.

States'rights was the main concern of this speech. Thomas
quoted from the Constitution: "the powers not delegated to
the United States by the Constitution, nor prohibited by it to
the States, are reserved to the States respectively or to the
people." He elaborated upon this and said that the powers
delegated to Congress did not include the promotion or the
exclusion of slavery; that was reserved for the States, and
as the California and New Mexico territories were acquired
by the joint effort of all of the States and were the property
of the States collectively, Congress could impose no prohibitions or laws that interfered with state sovereignty. Slavery
existed universally, sanctioned by no laws; where any law on
slavery existed it was for the prohibition of slavery, and only
in the states north of the Missouri compromise line. In closing
the speech, the impression was left that this line should be
maintained through the territories also.

May 27. Henry Bennett.

Speech of Hon. Henry Bennett, of New York, On the Admission of California. Delivered in the House of Representatives, Monday, May 27, 1850. Washington: Printed at the
Congressional Globe Office. 1850.

16 pp.

Bennett replied to some of the objections to the admi;ssion
of California.

The fact that a population of 70,680 entitles her to be admitted and half again as much or 106,021 entitles her to two
representatives, answered the census objection, as it was
generally assumed that by this time her population was well
over 100,000. "Both Florida and Michigan were admitted
without a census being taken; and for the same reason — it
being generally known that their population was sufficient."
Texas was again compared to California to answer the objection of large size. "California has no disputed or unsettled
boundaries . . . Is it not, then, her right to be admitted entire,
without division; . . . Would those [Southerners] opposing her
admission be more willing to admit two States than one?"
"I am for the immediate admission of California, and utterly
opposed to connecting with her admission the settlement of
the disputed boundary of Texas and New Mexico, or of the
exciting and agitating question in regard to slavery—."

June 3.   Williamson R. W. Cobb.
The Slavery Question. Speech of Mr. W. R. W. Cobb, of
Alabama, in the House of Representatives, June 3, 1850, in
Committee of the Whole on the state of the Union, on the
President's message relating to California.
Printed in the Congressional Globe, no separate seen.
"I am for the admission of California. But at the same time,
whilst I mete out justice to California, I shall ask that justice
be done to the residue of the newly-acquired territory, by the
organization of territorial Governments, upon the principle of
non-intervention, and by hearing and respecting the prayers
of the people in said territories, as well as of those in California."

June 3.   Thomas S. Bocock.
Admission of California. Speech of Mr. Bocock, of Virginia,
in the House of Representatives, June 3, 1850. Upon the difficulty between the North and the South upon the Slavery
Question.
8 pp. Caption title.
"My objections to voting for the admission of California

as a State, under her present constitution, if not absolutely
insuperable are very great. If the citizens of that territory,
acting by virtue of authority regularly granted, and in pur-
suance of prescribed form, had made a constitution excluding
slavery, we could have acquiesced. But this constitution is
based upon usurpation and revolution. At the ratification of
the treaty of Guadalupe Hidalgo, the sovereignty over this
territory passed into the people of the several States. They
could have ceded it, or any part of it, away again immediately
to raise the money to be paid to Mexico. From them that
sovereignty could never pass except by their consent given
by their agents or revolution. Their consent has never been
given; but on the contrary has been refused, expressly at the
time when the last Congress refused to pass a bill to allow
the people of California to form a State constitution. It is, then,
a case of revolution."

June 3.   William F. Colcok.

Speech of Mr. William F. Colcock, of South Carolina, on the
California Question. Delivered in the House of Representatives, June 3, 1850. Washington: Printed by Jno. T. Towers.
1850.

16 pp.

Unlike most of the speeches, Colcock did not deviate from
the subject, except in his closing remarks.

He spent much time speaking upon the procedures of Gener-
als Mason and Riley in California that resulted in the formation of a state government. He condemned the whole
procedure, along with President Taylor for his part in what
Colcock believed to have initiated it. Taylor was also condemned for not suggesting a southern boundary for the proposed State along the Missouri compromise line. "I must remind
gentlemen, that if California can assume the right to come
into the Union, any other State may assume the right peaceably
to go out of it."

He dwelt some on the compromise bill and concluded: "that
which is conceded to the North is performed; the little that is
conceded to the South is promised only. Her rights are left

in doubt."

June 3.   John Crowell.

On the Admission of California into the Union. Speech of Mr.
J. Crowell, of Ohio, in the House of Representatives, June 3,
1850. In Committee of the Whole on the state of the Union,
on the President's Message relating to California. (Printed
at the Congressional Globe Office.)

16 pp. Caption title.

The major portion of this speech was a diatribe on the
institution of slavery, not only against its extension, but
condemning it in the places where it already exists.

Crowell was favorable to the admission of California, "unembarrassed with any other subject of legislation, with its
present boundaries and its glorious free constitution." In concluding he stated: "The popular voice demands her instant
and unconditional admission, and bids us cease our profitless
discussions and proceed with the public business, now so long
and so ruinously delayed."

June 3.   Peter H. Silvester.

Speech of Mr. P. H. Silvester, of New York, on the Terri-
torial Question, the Admission of California, and for the
Union. Delivered in the House of Representatives of the
United States, June 3, 1850. Washington: Gideon & Co.,
Printers, 1850.

15 pp.

The major portion of this speech was anti-slavery in character, with much quoting from the speeches of other Congressmen to gain his points.

He did mention, in answer to objections to the admission
of California, that of 12,061 votes that were cast for her
constitution, not one was a foreign vote. There were 10,700
American and 1,300 Californian voters, who had elected to
become American citizens under the treaty, or Mexicans who
were obliged to leave Mexico because they favored the American cause.

He questioned the charges that President Taylor interfered

in, or promoted, the adoption of the constitution of California
excluding slavery from that State, on the grounds that the
President, most of his cabinet, and T. Butler King, the agent
who was sent to California by the President, were slave-
holders.

June 4. Walter Booth.

Speech of Hon. Walter Booth, of Connecticut, in the House
of Representatives. June 4, 1850, In Committee of the Whole
on the state of the Union, on the President's Message transmitting the Constitution of California. (Printed and for sale
by Buell & Blanchard, Sixth Street, south Pennsylvania Ave.
Price 50 cts, per 100.)

7 pp. Caption title.

Booth was strong in his abolitionistic views. He answered
various objections to the admission of California.

"Is it the distance of her location from the rest of the fami-
ly? Not at all. She is a neighbor of Oregon. Is it that she has
not a population sufficient to form a respectable State? . . .
the tide of emigration thither is flowing in such rapid currents,
as to give assurance that her present growth is, and that her
growth will be, without a precedent in this or any other
country. Is it because her inhabitants are not sufficiently
enlightened for self-government? Look at the Constitution she
has formed, and I fear not to affirm, that no gentleman will
hazard his reputation so much as to bring this objection against
her. Is it because her boundaries are too large? . . . It would
be a strange spectacle, indeed, to see gentlemen strangle at
California, who could swallow the empire or Republic of
Texas without inconvenience . . . What then is the cause of
delay? . . . the expectation of the Southern portion of these
States, that slavery would be extended over a part, if not the
whole of it . . . I stand here, sir, the advocate of the immediate
admission of California alone; without any entangling al-
liances."

June 4. John L. Taylor.

Admission of California. Speech of the Hon. John L. Taylor,

of Ohio, on the California and Territorial Questions: Delivered
in the House of Representatives of the United States, June 4,
1850. Washington: Gideon & Co., Printers. 1850.

14 pp.

This was a mild speech, seemingly to extol the action of
President Taylor in the California matter. Taylor quoted from
the President's California message in striving to exonerate
him of any complicity in the formation of the State's government.

"I am now ready and willing to vote for the admission of
California into the Union as one of the States of this Confederacy, with her constitution as her people have formed it
and with the limits and boundaries therein designated."

June 4. John A. King.

Speech of Mr. John A. King, of New York, on the Admission
of California; delivered in the House of Representatives, June
4, 1850. Washington: Gideon & Co., Printers. 1850.

15 pp.

"Let California be received, let her come alone; it is due
to usage, to her people, to her rights as a sovereign State; for
such she is, and can never be less."

June 4. Kinsley S. Bingham.

Speech of Mr. Bingham, of Michigan, on the Admission of
California. Delivered in the House of Representatives, June 4,
1850. Washington: Printed at the Congressional Globe Office.
1850.

22 pp.

Bingham plunged into the slavery question immediately
quoting lavishly from letters, resolutions and other speeches.
He began by quoting Jefferson in 1774, and other great slave-
holding statesmen of that generation, proving that they were
in favor of abolition. But that generation has gone and the
attitude has completely reversed itself in the South. The
references to California were but slight.

"I trust it will inspire them [his descendants] with an honest
pride to be able to say 'he opposed the extension of slavery'."

June 5. Jacob Thompson.
  Speech of Hon. Jacob Thompson, of Mississippi, on the California Question. Delivered in the House of Representatives,
June 5, 1850. (Towers, Print.)
    8 pp. Caption title.
  The speech was imbued with pro-slavery ideas and arguments. Thompson could not see his way to vote for the admission of California into the Union without compromise. He
was strongly in favor of the extension of the Missouri compromise line to the Pacific, making it the southern boundary of
California, and advocated the establishment of a territorial
government for "South California", with no prohibition of
slavery and entire freedom of the people to decide this question
when she applied for admission as a state.

June 5. Moses Hoagland.
  Speech of Hon. M. Hoagland, of Ohio, on the proposition to
Admit California as a State into the Union. Delivered in the
House of Representatives, June 5, 1850. Washington: Printed
at the Congressional Globe Office. 1850.
    7 pp.
  Hoagland was not inclined to favor anything attached to
the admission of California bill. Although he praised the
Congress for its spirit of compromise, he believed that the
rights and wants of the people in any of the territories should
be given first consideration by Congress to the exclusion of
all measures of compromise and related, or unrelated bills. He
felt that Congress has not the power to change any existing
laws, whether passed by the people, or a former government,
if they conform to our Constitution, and particularly in the
matter of slavery.

June 5. Andrew Johnson.
  The Admission of California. Speech of Mr. A. Johnson, of
Tennessee, in the House of Representatives, June 5, 1850.
    Printed in the Congressional Globe, no separate seen.
  Johnson said nothing upon the admission of California, but
directed most of his speech to and about the Representative

from Massachusetts, Winthrop, in very unflattering terms. Ashmun, from the same state, was not omitted, nor were their constituents, to whom he referred as "this Boston codfish aristocracy."

June 5. Finis E. McLean.
Admission of California. Speech of Hon. Finis E. McLean, of Kentucky, in the House of Representatives, June 5, 1850. In Committee of the Whole on the state of the Union, on the President's Message transmitting the constitution of California. (Printed at the Congressional Globe Office.)
   7 pp. Caption title.
"To admit California will be rather a risking policy. She would be a wild sister and very far from home. But for the sake of compromise and adjustment of the present difficulties, I would be willing to risk her. Perhaps we may be able to get along with her alone as a new State, but to bring in hastily a whole litter of such, and some of them less prepared, I cannot consent." It was his suggestion that Congress admit California and erect governments for the territories without a slavery proviso.

June 5. Cyrus L. Dunham.
Admission of California. Speech of Hon. C. L. Dunham, of Indiana, in the House of Representatives, Wednesday, June 5, 1850. In Committee of the Whole on the state of the Union, on the President's Message transmitting the Constitution of California. (Printed at the Congressional Globe Office.)
   14 pp.
The aim of this speech was almost obscured by a thunderous cloud of anti-Southern oratory. California was hardly mentioned but the main object of the speech was to induce the House to keep the new territories free of slavery.

June 5. John W. Howe.
Speech of J. W. Howe, of Pennsylvania, on the California question. Made in the House of Representatives, Night Session, June 5, 1850. (Buell & Blanchard, Printers.)

8 pp. Caption title.

Howe was an outspoken Whig and Free-soiler, strong in his conviction that there shall be no more slave states, although he accepted the possibility that under the agreement with Texas wherein she might divide herself into five states, these would allow slavery.

He objected to any bill or compromise being stuck onto the admission of California bill. He berated his Southern contemporaries for their attempts in this direction, along with Northerners who would accede to compromises. "I go for her unconditional admission, without making her a pack-horse, upon which to lug in other matters pertaining to the security of property in their black people, and the extension of slavery."

June 6. Milo M. Dimmick.

The Slavery Question. Speech of Mr. M. M. Dimmick, of Pennsylvania, in the House of Representatives, Thursday, June 6, 1850.

Printed in the Congressional Globe, no separate seen.

"California the Golden Star of the West, should be received into the constellation of States. I regard her admission, finally, as one of my colleagues has said, a foregone conclusion, unless our southern friends shall so far forget their own true interests, as well as that of the country ... Her domain, although vast, is still considerably less than Texas, nor can she ever equal New York or Pennsylvania in population, power, wealth or resources ... Then let her be admitted as a distinct proposition, or united with territorial bills for New Mexico and Utah without the proviso, and she shall receive my vote."

He stated that he had a dislike for all legislation affecting the social condition of those who are not directly or indirectly represented. The peoples of the territories had not asked to invoke the power of Congress to prohibit or to introduce slavery. They were perfectly tranquil on this subject, having confidence in their own ability to take care of themselves.

"As to the Abolitionists, some of them are doubtless honest and sincere in their desires to see the emancipation of the African race; but the great majority of them are actuated by treasonable motives, looking to overthrow this Union . . . It cannot, with fairness, be said that the Free soilers are abolitionists . . . the Free soilers are opposed to all interference in the States where it now exists, against the extension of slavery over the newly-acquired territory, and for the application of the Wilmot proviso, prohibiting its introduction."

June 6. Richard K. Meade.

Speech of Hon. R. K. Meade, of Virginia. On the Admission of California as a State. Delivered in the House of Representatives, June 6, 1850. Washington: Printed at the Congressional Globe Office. 1850.

14 pp.

This was an impassioned pro-slavery speech with only slight references to California. "To the Pacific, then I say — to the Pacific. Your [Southerner's] future security depends entirely upon your own strength; secure to yourselves while you can, an empire. When California and New Mexico and Oregon are settled up with an anti-slavery population, the pressure will become too powerful for resistance. Keep this population in your front, and look to the southern portion of this continent as your exclusive domain."

June 6. Richard I. Bowie.

Speech of Hon. Richard I. Bowie, of Maryland, on the California Question. Delivered in the House of Representatives, June 6, 1850. Washington: Printed by John T. Towers. 1850.

15 pp.

The California question, in this speech, did not loom up with near the importance as did the slavery question in the District of Columbia. As Maryland had ceded the District to the United States, she was concerned about, and against, the threatened abolition of slavery in the District.

Bowie declared that under the Constitution, any citizen of Maryland had the right to enter any territory of the United States with all of his personal property. The territories belong to the several States of the Union and Congress c a n n o t rightfully pass any law to prevent a citizen from settling there with any and all of his property.

It is quite possible that Bowie had by this time surmised that California was to be admitted as a free state and he might as well accept that fact gracefully. He concluded his speech with the following sentiment: "The rising power of California may be a counterpoise to the increasing power of the North. What have we to fear from a great State on the Pacific? She will be our natural ally; she must have cotton and sugar from Mississippi and Texas. Her population will be no propagandists; they will find in her own borders, and isles of the ocean, verge and scope enough for the most expanded philanthropy."

June 6. Jesse C. Dickey.

Speech of Hon. Jesse C. Dickey, of Pennsylvania, in the House of Representatives, in reference to the Admission of California and the Subject of Slavery. Made in Committee of the Whole, June 6, 1850.

7 pp.

Dickey expressed himself distinctly, and without elaboration upon the two subjects in this rather short speech.

He spoke against slavery, and particularly the extension of it. He compared the border counties of Delaware, Virginia and Maryland, that are contiguous to free states, with the more remote counties in the same state, and asserted that the people in the first mentioned are more prosperous and happier than are their brethren in the more southern counties.

He pleaded for the admission of California, refuting some of the arguments against it, giving various reasons for supporting it. He stated that the Jesuits, who were the first missionaries; and the Franciscans, the successors, held title to lands from the Spanish crown which the settlers now occupy, and California should be placed in a postion to have legal courts to settle these land matters. (Note: The Jesuits had established no missions in Upper California, and Spain had issued no titles to land, only concessions for its use.)

"The amount of revenue which this Government has derived from California, for the first year is some $600,000, and the amount which it is supposed will be received the ensuing year will probably reach $2,000,000. This in itself is an argument for her admission, as powerful as the gold itself."

June 6. David Hubbard.

The Territorial Question. Speech of Hon. David Hubbard, of Alabama, in the House of Representatives, Thursday, June 6, 1850, in Committee of the Whole on the state of the Union, on the President's Message transmitting the Constitution of California. (Printed at the Congressional Globe Office.)

7 pp. Caption title.

"It has become my duty to tell this House what my constituents expect at your hands. They have paid their part in money, and done their share of fighting for this Mexican country, and expect me to get for them, as partners, part of the land upon which they may go, carry their property with them, own and enjoy it, and remain part of this Union, undisturbed in their rights . . . You have to give them their share, or you will repent it."

Hubbard attacked the abolitionist with considerable venom, and drew a word picture of slavery conditions in the South, which, if true, appeared quite rosy, compared to the condition and responsibilities of the free laborers in the North.

He offered nothing on the California question, and only mentioned it to say that an able bodied negro man is worth five hundred dollars in the mines, and will hire for a thousand dollars a year, which would increase the value of slaves throughout the South by three hundred dollars.

June 7. Robert W. Johnson.

The Slavery Question. Speech of Mr. R. W. Johnson, of Arkansas, in the House of Representatives, Friday, June 7, 1850. The House having under consideration, as in Committee of the Whole, the President's Message communicating the Constitution of California.

Printed in the Congressional Globe, no separate seen.

Johnson advocated a united South to combat the so-called aggression of the united North in the matter of the territories.

In his words, the Missouri compromise has been a "happy policy," which if continued would give the South about half of the new territory for the extension of slavery. The formation of the State of California reduced the half to about one-third, but still the "North declares, we not only shall not have one third, but shall not have one foot of it. The Government itself has lost affinity for, and become hostile to the South, as exemplified in the fraudulent formation of the California Constitution."

June 7. Charles Durkee

The California Question. Speech of Mr. Charles Durkee, of Wisconsin, in the House of Representatives, Friday, June 7, 1850. (Printed by Buel & Blanchard, not seen.)

A long winded speech, offering few convictions of his own. He admonished the House to admit California, and give New Mexico and Utah territorial governments and apply the Wilmot proviso thereto.

He mentioned the "wicked Florida war, . . . where the American name was disgraced, by shamelessly violating the flag of truce in the seizure of the noble-hearted Osceola . . . The Mexican war was similar in its origin, but more vast in extent, and in its enormities."

"The war now waged in these Halls, and throughout the Republic, is, in my opinion, conducted on Christian principles." Little did he realize that this "war" in which he was playing a part was even then festering into the bloodiest war of our past history, the Civil war.

June 7. George A. Caldwell.

California and the Territorial Questions. Speech of Mr. G. A. Caldwell, of Kentucky, in the House of Representatives, Friday, June 7, 1850.

Printed in the Congressional Globe, no separate seen.

"If we pass a bill that shall organize territorial governments for Utah and New Mexico, without the Wilmot proviso, I will consent to couple with it a bill for the immediate admission of California as a State into the Union, leaving her people

to determine the question of slavery for themselves, as the
people of every State have the unquestionable right to do."
      He stated that the present alarming state of things had its
origin long before the acquisition of California. Political parties
were first fully developed during the administration of the
elder Adams. The Republican party, now called the Democratic party, found its strength in the South, and was wedded
to the sovereign rights of the states, and insisted on restraining
the powers of the Federal Government within the limits of a
strict construction of the Constitution. "The Federal party,
(in the North) aiming at the establishment of a splendid
central government, sought by every ingenuity to enlarge the
powers granted in the Constitution, and by implication and
latitudinous constructions of that instrument, to derive and
exercise powers which the States and the people had never
granted."

June 7.   James H. Duncan.

Speech of Hon. J. H. Duncan, of Mass., on the California and
Territorial Questions. Delivered in the House of Representatives, June 7, 1850. Washington: Printed at the Congressional
Globe Office, 1850.
      8 pp.
      "I am in favor of the admission of California as a State
with her present constitution and proposed boundaries as a
separate and independent measure . . . Admit her to the Union,
and to a great extent you quiet the agitation of the country . . .
If the territorial bills are presented for the government of New
Mexico and Utah, I shall vote for the exclusion of slavery
from those territories . . . I look with confidence and trust for
the extinction of slavery."

June 8.   Fayette McMullen.

Admission of California. Speech of Mr. F. McMullen, of
Virginia, in the House of Representatives, Saturday, June 8,
1850.
      Printed in the Congressional Globe, no separate seen.
      There was little in this speech but an argument against the

Wilmot proviso, punctuated with expressions of ill-will toward
several members of the House.

In the course of an argument, he was asked point blank,
how he stood on the California question: "I shall most assured-
ly vote against the admission of California, unless she is
brought in connection with the settlement of other questions
in controversy."

June 8. John S. Phelps.

Admission of California. Speech of Mr. John S. Phelps, of
Missouri, (in the House) Saturday, June 8, 1850.

Printed in the Congressional Globe, no separate seen.

"In 1846, before the people of California were aware that
war existed between this country and Mexico, the American
settlers [the Bear Flag party, who were, according to Phelps,
mostly from Missouri] had conquered Upper California.
Colonel Frémont, with his exploring party, which had been
raised in Missouri, was at this time in Upper California. The
Mexican authorities had attempted to drive him and his party
from the country. He was invited to command the forces of
the insurgents. He accepted it. In a few days the Conquest of
California was accomplished. . . . The people of Missouri,
therefore, feel a deep interest — deeper than those of any
memeber of this Confederacy, in the question of the admission
of California into the Union. [This was a commendable and
patriotic thought, but history has reduced, somewhat, the
greatness of the military achievement.]

I should have been better pleased if the people of California had recognized slavery. But as I recognize the right of
the people of California to prohibit or establish slavery as
suits their pleasure, I submit."

Much of earlier Congressional action on the California
matter was given, and together with his own discussion of the
question, occupied about five-sixths of his alloted time, the
rest of the time was devoted to other measures of the Clay
compromise.

June 8.   John McQueen.

Speech of Hon. John McQueen, of S. Carolina, on the admission of California. Delivered in the House of Representatives June 3 [sic], 1850. Washington: Printed at the Congressional Globe Office. 1850.

11 pp.

There is only a half page in the printed speech with any reference to California and the other territories. The balance of the speech was a strong pro-slavery argument.

He referred to the inhabitants of California as a "floating population of every color and nation" and insisted that the un-American population, according to the Constitution can only be citizens after five years, and that Congress give California a territorial government along with the rest of the territory. "This whole thing of the sovereign State of California would look better in the pages of the Arabian Nights than the archives of this body."

June 8.   Chester Butler.

Speech of Hon. Chester Butler, of Penn., on the Admission of California; delivered in the House of Representatives of the United States, June 8, 1850. Washington: Gideon & Co., printers. 1850.

28 pp.

As the Constitution fixed the representative ratio of slaves as three-fifths of the whole and as it is no longer legal to import slaves, slaves taken into new territories must then be taken from the Slave States, then there could be no additional representation in the House for the Slave States. "Let the slaves and slave territory be where they are and as they are and free territory where it is and as it is."

Slavery was recognized by the Constitution as a local institution in fifteen states, each with varying laws regarding it, and none of these laws can extend under the Constitution to the shores of the Pacific.

"I am ready to vote for the admission of California. I would still go one step further, and vote for a bill admitting California and forming territorial governments for the territories,

provided it could be so guarded, as not to give the Southern
side of the question any advantage of fact or argument. . . ."

June 8. William T. Hamilton.

Admission of California. Speech of Hon. W. T. Hamilton, of
Maryland, in the House of Representatives, June 8, 1850. In
Committee of the Whole on the state of the Union, on the
President's Message in relation to the admission of California.
(Printed at the Congressional Globe Office.)

8 pp. Caption title.

Hamilton acknowledged that "the destiny of California is
fixed. . . Admit California, and provide for the establishment
of governments for the balance of the territory, unrestricted
and untrammeled by provisos and you dispose of the question
now stirring the people." In his judgement the South could
gain nothing by opposing the admission. If she is refused admission at this time, it will only be a short time before she
will again be knocking at the door of Congress with her same
constitution and its anti-slavery clause.

June 8. John R. Thurman.

Speech of Hon. J. R. Thurman, of New York, on the California Question. Delivered in the House of Representatives,
Saturday, June 8, 1850. Washington: Printed at the Congressional Globe Office. 1850.

8 pp.

This speech was mostly upon the extension of slavery into
the territories, and the power of Congress to exclude it therefrom. Thurman aligned himself with the President's recommendation for the admission of California as she presented
herself to Congress, but was not in favor of the Congress
establishing territorial governments for the residual territories
without prohibiting slavery.

June 10. Thomas H. Benton.

Mr. Benton's Anti-compromise Speech. Speech of Mr. Benton,
of Missouri, in the Senate of the United States, June 10, 1850.
On his motion to postpone until the 4th day of March 1851,

the bill reported from the Committee of Thirteen, — the Compromise Bill.

15 pp. Caption title.

This is the third speech by Benton within two months on the same subject. Half of it dealt with the Texas boundary difficulty, and on the California question, but little was added to what was already spoken on April 8.

Benton represented a slave-holding state, and by all political concepts, should have lent his weight with his Southern colleagues in the matter of compromises attached to the California bill, but no doubt, his judgement was tempered by the fact that his son-in-law, Frémont, was the Senator elect from California, and was impatiently pacing the threshold of Congress waiting to be admitted with his State.

June 10. John A. McClernand.

The California Question. Speech of Mr. J. A. McClernand, of Illinois, in the House of Representatives, Monday, June 10, 1850.

Printed in the Congressional Globe, no separate seen.

Although representing a northern state, McClernand had ill-concealed contempt for the Wilmot proviso and its author. He said that the insistent threat of the proviso had done great damage to the progress of amelioration and emancipation of the slave under the benign laws of God and humanity, particularly in Virginia and Maryland, where slavery was just lingering, and also in Kentucky and Missouri, where it was expected to disappear at no very distant day. Instead it has converted the cause of humanity into an angry question of sectional political power. "It would have violated the Constitution, crippled the treaty-making power, aggressed upon the rights of the States, invited foreign and even inimical intervention in our domestic affairs, in fine, would have envolved us in infinite difficulty and ridicule. . . I accord to him all the glory of its authorship."

He prepared a bill, had it printed, and placed upon the members tables.

1.   For the admission of California.

2. For the territorial government of Utah.

3. For the territorial government of New Mexico.

4. For the arrangement of the northern boundary of Texas.
"I am prepared to vote for it in its present form, or with the
Texas boundary stricken out."

June 10. Marshall J. Wellborn.

The California and Territorial Questions. Speech of Mr. M.
J. Wellborn, of Georgia, in the House of Representatives,
June 10, 1850.

Printed in the Congressional Globe, no separate seen.

Wellborn once more advocated the extension of the Missouri
compromise line to the Pacific, "Perhaps the most inveterate
objection to this plan is, that its application would divide the
boundaries of California." He claimed that the Government
has the discretionary right to adjust the boundaries of territorial applicants for membership into the "Confederacy."

June 10. Thaddeus Stevens.

Speech of Thaddeus Stevens, of Pennsylvania, on the California Question. Made in the House of Representatives, Night
Session, June 10, 1850. (Buell & Blanchard, Printers.)

8 pp. Caption title.

The speech was opened by a discussion of the powers of
Congress over the territories, but soon resolved itself into a
diatribe against slavery and its Representatives. There was
hardly a mention of California.

"That an independent nation [Texas], without treaty and
without warrant in the Constitution, by a mere act of Congress,
was corruptly admitted into this Confederacy for the avowed
purpose of extending the dominion of slavery; and that California and New Mexico were acquired for the same object."
Although lacking in grammatical construction, this conveys a
fact that history often eludes.

June 10. Sampson W. Harris.

Speech of the Hon. Sampson W. Harris, of Alabama, on the
Measures of Compromise. Delivered in the House of Repre-

sentatives, June 10, 1850. (Towers Print.)

16 pp. Caption title.

"I am opposed, sir, to the admission of California as a State, into the Union; not only because I regard the circumstances connected with her organization as grossly violative of the rights of the south, but as an open infraction of the fundamental law of the land."

Each measure of compromise was opposed in turn with fairly logical argument, at least from a Southern point of view.

June 10.   Meredith P. Gentry.

Speech of Mr. M. P. Gentry, of Tennessee, on the Admission of California. Delivered in the House of Representatives, Monday, June 10, 1850. (Gideon & Co., Printers.)

8 pp. Caption title.

Speech of M. P. Gentry, of Tenn., on the Admission of California, delivered in the House of Representatives, U. S., Monday, June 10, 1850. Washington: Gideon & Co., Printers. 1850.

15 pp.

A bland speech which was, more or less, a recapitulation of what had transpired in the House during the six months previous.

Gentry indicated his opinion by saying that the "causes which exist — and which legislation cannot change — make it impossible for slavery to obtain a permanent foothold in the Territories acquired from Mexico. The character and sentiments of the people who inhabit them, and who are likely to emigrate thither — the character of the country, its soil and climate, all conspire to make such a result impossible."

June 10.   David S. Kaufman.

The Slavery Question, and its adjustment. Speech of Mr. D. S. Kaufman, of Texas, (in the House) Monday, June 10, 1850.

Printed in the Congressional Globe, no separate seen.

Kaufman was a member of the nine composing the Committee on Territories. The speech was mostly on the Texas — New Mexico boundary. However, he did repeat measures of compromise that were offered to the House by him on February 18th, viz:

1. Admit California with her southern boundary on the Missouri compromise line:

2. Establish territorial governments without provisions regarding slavery:

3. Acknowledge the whole boundary claimed by Texas:

4. Extend the laws of Maryland regarding slavery over the District of Columbia:

5. More effective fugitive slave laws.

June 11.   Lewis Cass.

Speech of Mr. Cass, of Michigan, on the motion of Mr. Benton for the indefinite postponement of the Compromise Bill. Delivered in the Senate of the United States, June 14, [sic] 1850. (Towers, Print.)

16 pp. Caption title.

Even at this date, Cass was sure that the bill to admit California would fail if put to a vote in the Senate as an isolated measure, as every Southern Senator but one would vote agaist it. He argued that the bill for California and the compromises relative to the establishment of territorial governments for the residue of the acquisition from Mexico were allied, and that they should be passed together to settle the slavery agitation in this field once and for all times. If this was not done, there would be repetition of the agitation in the future.

June 11.   Volney E. Howard.

Speech of the Hon. V. E. Howard, of Texas, against the admission of California, and the dismemberment of Texas. Delivered in the House of Representatives, June 11, 1850, in the Committee of the Whole on the California Message. Washington: Gideon & Co., printers. 1850.

16 pp.

This man, being a Representative from Texas, had the audacity to remark that: "the justice of permitting a few persons thus to monopolize an empire [California] which they cannot occupy, to the expulsion of one half of the States of the Union, cannot readily be apprehended."

He pointed out that there are more important considerations in the best interest of California than statehood. In the matter of land titles, according to the report of William Carey Jones on this subject, there never has been a surveyor in California, and therefore no complete titles to land there which would allow no revenue from this source, thus the new State must of necessity call for Federal funds for support. He claimed that the people have no right to establish a state government without the sanction of Congress, for the reason that the framers of that constitution were not citizens of California, but citizens of other states, or foreigners who have not the right to ask for admission.

Nearly half of this speech was upon the California question, and was one of the few speeches of the time that did not digress from the subjects at hand.

For all of his objections he came to California in 1853, to become active in politics and eventually a judge.

June 11, 12. William L. Dayton.

Speech of Mr. Dayton, of N. J., on the Compromise Bill: Delivered in the Senate of the United States, June 11 and 12, 1850.

16 pp. Caption title.

The California question was ignored. The Texas — New Mexico difficulty and Utah were the subjects on the first day.

Even a month before California came knocking at the door of Congress, Utah applied for admission as a state under the name of Deseret. It proposed to include all of the territory acquired by the Mexican war east of the Sierra Nevadas from Oregon to the Mexican border, San Diego and a part of Southern California with Salt Lake City as the seat of government. With the excitement that California caused in Congress, Deseret received no attention until now. The cause was hopeless. The size was too large, and any smaller portion of this area would not contain sufficient population, and it is evident that the Mormons at this time were not looked upon with much respect. "We recollect the scenes which took place

in Missouri and Illinois, and unless their morals and manners
have improved, (if what were then said of them be true,) so
far from their needing protection against the Indians, the
Indians may soon have better cause to demand protection
against them; still protection against the Indians requires a
military force only, and protection they should have."

June 20.   John M. Berrien.
(Speech of Berrien, of Georgia, in the Senate.)
Printed in the Congressional Globe as part of a debate,
with no caption, no separate seen.
"Is California entitled to two Representatives in the other
branch of Congress? Are the persons chosen as Senators and
Representatives by the occupants of the public domain in
California and the Mexican residents there entitled to seats
in the Congress of the United States?"
Based upon reports, Berrien speculated the population to be
about 75,000 or 85,000. "From this is to be deducted transient
American citizens, who were there for temporary purposes,
retaining their domicils in the United States. But that the population fell very much below this estimate, I think is ascertained
by the fact that the vote upon so important a question as the
adoption of the constitution was limited to fifteen thousand,
a fraction above twelve thousand voting for it. One of two
conclusions appears to me to be indisputable. Either the number
of the population is vastly overrated, or that the constitution
is not the expression of the will of a majority of that people."

June 24, 25.   Pierre Soulé.
(Speech of Soulé, of Louisiana, in the Senate.)
Printed in the Congressional Globe as part of a debate, with
no caption, no separate seen.
Soulé spoke upon the amendment he offered to the Califor-
nia admission bill.
"Be it enacted, &c., that as soon as California shall have
passed in convention an ordinance providing — "
That she relinquish all title to public domain.
That she will not impede any control which the United

States may exercise over mining regions, etc.

That the lands of non-residents shall never be taxed higher than those of residents.

That navigable waters shall be open and free.

That the southern limits shall be restricted to the Missouri compromise line.

That the country lying below 36° 30' shall constitute a territory under the name of South California.

June 26 and 28.   Stephen A. Douglas.

Speech of Mr. Douglas, of Illinois, in reply to Mr. Soulé, relative to the Public Lands in California. Delivered in the Senate of the United States, June 26th and 28th, 1850. Washington: Printed at the Congressional Globe Office. 1850.

14 pp.

Although this speech is entirely on the matter of public lands, it hinges on the prospect of California becoming a state.

"How have you fulfilled your treaty stipulations? The only law you have extended to her is the taxing power; the only administrators of justice you have sent her are the taxgatherers. You leave her citizens without protection as to life, as to property; as to person;; you refuse to furnish money to bear her expenses; you refuse to give her that protection which all other people in the United States have received at your hands, at the same time you extract hundreds of thousands of dollars from her through your custom-houses;."

June 27.   Daniel Webster.

(Speech of Webster, of Massachusetts, in the Senate:)

Printed in the Congressional Globe as part of a debate, with no caption, no separate seen.

Webster voiced his disapproval of the Soulé amendment. To have this amendment sent to California for action there would delay her admission further, and to this, he was not agreeable. He objected to some of the sections of the amendment, particularly the erecting of South California. "And what is the value of South California disconnected from North California? . . . You have mountains, and you have those vast tracts of land east of the mountains. . . . eight months in every year roll on without a drop of rain falling, and there is not within the whole of it any land whatever that can be cultivated without irrigation."

June 27.   Henry S. Foote.
Speech of Hon. H. S. Foote, of Mississippi, on the Measures of Compromise. Delivered in the Senate of the United States, June 27, 1850. (Towers, printer.)

16 pp.

"It seems to be generally understood that the amendment now under consideration is virtually what is known as the Missouri Compromise. As I design to vote for this amendment, although I feel thoroughly persuaded that it is impossible it can obtain the sanction of this body or that of the other house of the National legislature."

He stated that he will vote against the admission of California if it is offered as a separate measure. If the compromise fails, as an alternative he considered the extension of the Missouri compromise line to California. It was a consideration of last resort, as he was not favorable to the geographical line in itself, and read from various speeches of Calhoun and a Jefferson letter pointing to the fact that they also were not favorable to the line.

June 27, 28.   Jefferson Davis.
(Speech of Davis, of Mississippi, in the Senate.)

Printed in the Congressional Globe as part of a debate, with no caption, no separate seen.

Davis had not said very much on the California question or on the Clay compromise. He was willing to vote for it even though he did not approve of all of it. He mentioned as much in this speech.

"What have we in Mississippi to be advantaged by the creation of territorial governments which do not recognize our right to migrate with our private property — . . . I can have no motive save to provide for the people of those remote districts the protection of territorial governments . . . far better for me is it, as a southern man, to admit California as a separate bill, and save the whole of Texas for the future increase of southern strength."

June 28, 29. John Davis.

Speech of Mr. Davis, of Massachusetts, on the Compromise Bill. Delivered in the Senate of the United States, June 28th and 29th, 1850. Washington: Printed at the Congressional Globe Office. 1850.

16 pp.

"The first portion of this bill makes provision for the introduction of California as a State into this Union. That is a measure, sir, which meets my approbation, and I am anxiously desirous to give my cordial support. . . I have supposed that there was a population there which was sufficient in number, sufficient in respectability, and sufficient in intelligence to manage a State organization with advantage to themselves and usefulness to the whole country. That, sir, is one great reason why she should be admitted."

Toward the rest of the compromise bill he was not so agreeable. "It seems to me that it contains concessions on but one side, and that does not amount to compromise."

June 29, July 1. James Cooper.

(Speech of Cooper, of Pennsylvania, in the Senate.)

Printed in the Congressional Globe as part of a debate, with no caption, no separate seen.

Cooper said that the principal object of the President, as appeared in his message of January 21st, was to get rid of the Wilmot proviso and the conflict and exasperation, which he feared that measure would raise. At that time, the opposition to the admission of California was not as violent as later, and the New Mexico — Texas boundary collision had not yet occured.

"If there were in the condition and circumstances of California, at the time she formed her State government, reasons to justify her in the act, the same reasons, with other superadded, appeal to us now in favor of the prompt admission into the Union. Her cities have become seats of a large and growing commerce; already disputes have arisen between the Government collector and the officers of the local authorities. The public domain within her limits requires regulation; and the people need the protection of law to secure them in the full enjoyment of their rights. It is true, they have formed a State government, . . . But recognize it, give to it the sanction of Congress, admit the State into the Union, and it will give force and efficiency to the government."

July 1, 2. William Upham.
(Speech of Upham, of Vermont, in the Senate.)
Printed in the Congressional Globe as part of a debate, with no caption, no separate seen.
In this rather long speech the history of the Ordinance 1787 appears to be the main subject, but which has its bearing on the territorial question of 1850, and at which it is aimed.
As to California, Upham wanted the bill for her admission offered separately, entirely divorced from other measures. He spoke as if there was some doubt in his mind about California being admitted with her offered constitution, and proceeded to give several arguments favoring her admission and prohibition of slavery there. He saw that there was yet danger of slavery being introduced, and read into his speech the following advertisement which appeared in the "Mississippian" of March 7, 1850.
"California — The Southern Slave Colony. Citizens of the slave States, desirous of emigrating to California with their slave property, are requested to send their names, number of slaves, and period of contemplated departure, to the address of Southern Slave Colony, Jackson, Mississippi.
All letters, to meet with attention, must be post paid.
It is the desire of the friends of this enterprise to settle in the richest mining and agricultural portion of California, and to secure their uninterrupted enjoyment of slave property. It is estimated that by the first of May next, the members of the Slave Colony will amount to about five thousand, and the slaves to about ten thousand. [Etc.]"

July 2. William H. Seward, of New York.

Speech of William H. Seward, on the Compromise bill: Delivered in the Senate of the United States, July 2, 1850.
(Gideon & Co., Printers.)

  15 pp. Caption title.

  Seward was emphatically unfavorable towards the compromise bill. He saw it as an injustice to all sections of the
Country. The admission of California should not be dependent
upon the establishment of territorial governments for New
Mexico and Utah, the Texas — New Mexico boundary dispute, nor the slavery question in the District of Columbia.
None of these should be tied together as a compromise bill,
but should be offered for consideration as separate issues. They
were finally offered separately.

July 3, 5. John Bell.

The Compromise Bill. Speech of Hon. John Bell, of Tennessee,
in the Senate of the United States, July 3 and 5, 1850. On the
Bill for the admission of California into the Union, the establishment of Territorial Governments for Utah and New
Mexico, and making proposals to Texas for the settlement of
her northern boundaries.

  24 pp. Caption title.

  This was in support of his compromise bill, offered February
28. The bill proposed to form two new States out of Texas:
To pay Texas for her territorial claims against New Mexico:
Allow New Mexico to establish a State government, without
slavery restrictions: Admit California: Set up a territorial
government for the residue of the Mexican war acquisition
without slavery restrictions.

  Although the speech was quite long it was evidently listened
to with intense interest. It was interrupted fifty-seven times,
and developed many arguments of a more or less trivial nature.

July 5, 6. John Bell.

Speech of John Bell, of Tennessee, on Slavery in the United
States, and the causes of the present dissensions between the
North and the South. Delivered in the Senate of the United

States on the 5th and 6th of July, 1850. Washington: Gideon
and Co., Printers. 1850.

30 pp.

This being a continuation of the speech that commenced
two days before.

As the title indicates, the speech was upon slavery, but the
main subject of the newly acquired territories, that was before
the Senate, was not entirely omitted.

With the advent of Polk to the Presidency, "he prosecuted
the claim of United States to the whole of Oregon with a
vigor which well-nigh involved the country in a war with
Great Britain. But that danger passed, and the possession of
Oregon with its present boundaries secured — either from
the necessities of his position, or upon some calculation of
glory, he unhesitatingly, and with the cordial support of his
followers, north and south, plunged his country into a war
with Mexico; indicating from the commencement, by circumstances unmistakable, that it would not be terminated without
a further acquisition of territory.   The annexation of Texas
just consummated, accompanied by a stipulation for the admission of three or four slave states to be carved out of her
territory; and then, following close upon the heels of that
measure, a scheme for the further acquisition of territory in
the same quarter, gave new activity to every anti-slavery
sentiment and prejudice at the North."

The Democrats, the party in power, congratulated themselves upon the results of the Mexican war, but it was not
long before the "Southern Democracy, especially, began to
suspect that in the acquisition of California and New Mexico
they had got what they did not expect, and did not want — a
vast accession of territory in which slavery was practically
forbidden by the unalterable laws of nature, if not human
laws."

July 8. Truman Smith.

Speech of Mr. Smith, of Conn., on the Bill "To admit California into the Union — to establish Territorial Governments
for Utah and New Mexico, making proposals to Texas for

the establishment of the Western and Northern Boundaries;"
showing the responsibilities of the late Administration on
account of the acquisitions which were the result of our recent
war with Mexico — [etc.]. Delivered in the Senate of the
United States, July 8, 1850. Washington: Gideon & Co.,
Printers. 1850.

   32 pp.

This appears to be the longest speech on the subject. It
included many statistics and excerpts.

Smith put the blame on President Polk for the turbulent
agitation growing out of the territorial acquisitions from Mexico in the late war. If Polk had heeded the warning given
him before the close of the war, some from the floor of
Congress and some from ten Northern States and three
Southern States, and had settled the southern boundary of the
ceded territory on the Missouri compromise line of 36° 30',
the slavery agitation and the Texas — New Mexico boundary
difficulty would not have existed. This would have given the
United States the San Francisco harbor and most of the gold
producing region, which at that time, was considered the only
important or valuable section.

In concluding his speech, he gave much credit and praise
to President Taylor for his handling of the California situation
and other problems. Smith was not aware that during his
speech, news was brought to the Senate that the President
had taken a turn for the worse in his illness. The President
died the next day, July 9, 1850.

July 9, 15. Arthur P. Butler.

The Compromise Bill. Speech of Mr. Butler, of South Carolina,
in the Senate, Tuesday, July 9 [and 15], 1850.

Printed in the Congressional Globe, no separate seen.

The Senate was recessed from the 9th until the 15th on
account of the death of President Taylor. Butler finished his
speech on the 15th.

To admit California with her "present" limits and under
the circumstances, Butler regarded as unconstitutional. He
promoted the argument that California in its proposed size

was too large, and included a population that would give her more representation in Congress than was agreeable to him. He proposed that she be curtailed by establishing her southern limit on 36° 30', the Missouri compromise line. He was not entirely satisfied with the Missouri compromise in that it forbade Southerners with slaves north of that line, but gave equal rights to both Northerners and Southerners south of that line.

July 17.   Daniel Webster, of Massachusetts.
Speech of the Honorable Daniel Webster, on the Compromise Bill, delivered in the Senate of the United States, on the 17th day of July, 1850. Washington: Gideon & Co., Printers. 1850.
28 pp. Printed wrapper.
Same (Gideon & Co., Printers.)
15 pp. Caption title.

By this time it was acknowledged that California would be admitted into the Union as a state. The question now became as to whether she should be voted in on a separate bill, or as part of a compromise bill effecting territorial governments for New Mexico and Utah. Webster was of the opinion that the California bill should not be separate. He ascertained from Douglas, chairman of the committee on territories, that the moment the California bill was disposed of, the territorial bill would be offered. This, Webster felt, would only prolong the bitter agitation. Any anti-slavery provision in the proposed territorial governments would not pass in the Senate, as the pro-slavery and anti-slavery forces were in equal number, but without this provision the bill would not pass in the House, as the majority there were from the North.

"What is now proposed, is, to make a territorial government for New Mexico and Utah, without [slavery] restriction. . . . I have voted against restriction for the reason which I have already given to the Senate [speech of March 7] . . . I shall never consent to end this session of Congress until some provision be made for New Mexico. Utah is less important. Let her repose herself upon the borders of the Salt Lake another year, if necessary."

July 17. Thomas H. Bayly.
 Speech of Hon. T. H. Bayly, of Virginia, on the proceedings
 of the Executive in California and New Mexico. Delivered in
 the House of Representatives, Wednesday, August [sic] 17,
 1850. Washington: Printed at the Congressional Globe Office.
 1850.
      15 pp.
 It has been said that Taylor did not at any time during his
campaign for the Presidency, or thereafter, declare himself
upon the issue of slavery in the new territories. Bayly said that
he was held up at the North as a friend of the Wilmot proviso,
which if applied to these territories would prohibit slavery,
and at the South as its most reliable opponent. In order to
appease the North, evade responsibility and embarassment to
the party, he induced the Californians to apply for statehood
with a constitution prohibiting slavery. This certainly seems
to fit the picture, but the President's influence in the formation
of the State was actually of little consequence. In Bayly's
opinion California was admirably suited to African slavery.
"It is warmer than eastern Virginia, and there is no pursuit
in which slave labor can be so well employed as in mining,"
but the threat of the Wilmot proviso, and the shortage of
slaves in the South dissuaded the slaveholder from going there.

July 18. Robert M. T. Hunter.
 Speech of Hon. R. M. Hunter, of Virginia. [In the Senate.]
   16 pp. Caption title.
   "I am called upon to vote for the admission of California
 with an anti-slavery constitution, which was not the result,
 as I believe, of her people, but the action, direct and indirect,
 of the General Government . . . How can I vote for such a
 bill?"
   This was a long, tedious dissertation on the effect the
compromise bill would have upon slavery in the Territories of
Utah and New Mexico if passed. He was not pleased to have
Texas give up any territorial claims to New Mexico, because
if there were no positive laws regarding slavery in these territories, no slave-holder would venture there with his property,

and all would eventually become free soil.

July 19. George W. Jones.
Iowa and the Compromise Bill. Remarks of Mr. Jones, of Iowa, in the Senate, July 19, 1850.

Printed in the Congressional Globe, no separate seen.

"Anxious as I am for the admission of California, I am unwilling that it should be done, and the other sores on the body-politic left to fester, and ultimately, perhaps to destroy the whole system, when the means of healing all at once are at our own command, and can be safely and advantageously applied. The people of the territories are quite as much, and in my opinion more in need of the fostering care, of the parent Government than those of California are, they now having an organized government, and the number and strength to support themselves."

July 22. Henry Clay.
Speech of Mr. Clay, of Kentucky, on Measures of Compromise. Delivered in the Senate of the United States, July 22, 1850. Washington: Printed by Jno. T. Towers. 1850.

31 pp.

Once more Clay spoke for his compromise, but in more

length on each point. He felt, and said as much, that if this measure is defeated, the chairman of the Committee on Territories (Douglas) will call up the California bill separately, and it will pass by a majority in both Houses, and that "will have the unavoidable tendency of aggravating the sense of wrong and injury — whether well or ill-founded" that exists in the South.

The measure was dubbed "omnibus" because it provided for so many matters. "I thank, from the bottom of my heart, the enemy of the bill who gave it that denomination. The omnibus is the vehicle of the people, of the mass of people. And this bill deserves the name for another reason; that with the exception of the two bills which are to follow, it contains all that is necessary to give peace and quiet to the country."

Clay did not hesitate to give vent to his ideas and criticisms, and as a result drew more than one sharp retort from several Senators during the speech.

July 23.   David L. Yulee.
The Compromise Bill. Speech of Hon. D. L. Yulee, of Florida, in the Senate, July 23, 1850.
Printed in the Congressional Globe, no separate seen.
A debate upon the right of slave-holders to bring their property into the territories and the power of Congress to legislate upon this right.
This might be more rightly called an argument with Foote of Mississippi. There was little love lost between the two.

July 24.   David Wilmot.
The California Question. Speech of Hon. David Wilmot, of Pennsylvania, in the House of Representatives, Wednesday, July 24, 1850.
7 pp. Caption title.
Part of this speech was an attack upon McClernand in retaliation of that gentleman's remarks upon the Wilmot proviso on June 10th.
Wilmot was strongly in favor of the immediate admission of California. Of course he blamed the slave interests for the delay, but he condemned a few Northern men, particularly McClernand and Douglas for their expressions, that to Wilmot, allied them with the South.
On slavery, he remarked that the increase in the value of slaves had risen in the preceeding fifty years from two hundred millions to sixteen hundred millions of dollars. "I look forward to some day — remote it may be — when the South in its own way, and by its own voluntary action will set about the great work of emancipation. . . That day must come, or there will come a night of terror and blood."

July 24.   John A. McClernand.
The California Question. Remarks of Hon. J. A. McClernand, of Illinois, in the House of Representatives, Wednesday, July

24, 1850, in reply to the remarks of Mr. Wilmot.
Printed in the Congressional Globe, no separate seen.
McClernand repeated his stand on the California question
given in his speech of June 10. This was short and extempo-
raneous, but more of a counter-attack on Wilmot.

July 24. Edson B. Olds.
Speech of Hon. Edson B. Olds, of Ohio, on the California
question. Delivered in the House of Representatives, Wednesday, July 24, 1850. Washington: Printed at the Congressional
Globe Office. 1850.
    7 pp.
    "I regard it as a fixed fact, that California, unless connected
with other measures, will knock in vain for admission into the
American Union. The sin, sir, does not, and shall not lie at my
door. If a state was formed out of territory in which slavery
had a preëxistence, and whose constitution still recognized
its existence, I would cheerfully vote for her admission into
the Union. My opposition is not to the admission of slave
states, but to the extension of slavery into free territory."
    Little else was said about the California question. The rest
of his speech was taken up in denouncing the Whig party.

July 30. Harvey Putnam.
Admission of California. Speech of Harvey Putnam, of New
York, in the House of Representatives, Tuesday July 30, 1850,
In Committee of the Whole on the state of the Union, on the
bill making appropriations for the payment of Revolutionary
Pensioners. (Printed at the Congressional Globe Office.)
    8 pp. Caption title.
    On opening the speech, Putnam said: "On the motion just
made to lay aside the California message, in order to take up
appropriation bill, I voted in the negative. A majority, however,
has decided that the latter shall have preference."
    After a few remarks in favor of the appropriations, he
launched into a negative discussion upon the expansion of
slavery into the territories, and slavery in general. He made
it clear that he was not in favor of tacking any compromise

bills to the bill for the admission of California.

Aug. 1. Henry S. Foote.

Speech of Mr. Foote, of Mississippi, on the Admission of California. Delivered in the Senate of the United States, August 1, 1850. (Towers, Print.)

16 pp. Caption title.

"Now, sir, I, as a Missouri Compromise man, must say that the mere line of 36 deg. 30 min., as a line for the purpose of dividing the supposed landed estates of the North and the South respectively, is to me a great and ridiculous absurdity; and I call upon those who have heretofore united with me in supporting the Missouri Compromise, according to its ancient meaning, to join me once more in sustaining and enforcing it against all of the false teachers of the present hour." At this time in South Carolina there were several political agitators, Rhett and others, who were trying to make the Missouri compromise line an ultimatum; either the passage of it, or the dissolution of the Union. Foote soundly berated them.

The speech is entirely in this vein, with no allusion to the California question.

Aug. 2. George E. Badger.

(Speech of Badger, of North Carolina, in the Senate.)

Printed in the Congressional Globe as part of a debate, with no caption, no separate seen.

"I much prefer California, if admitted at all, admitted with the whole extent of boundary which she claims. I prefer it because, if we are to have a free State upon the Pacific, without any arrangement of compromise, or compensation, it is far better to have one than two free States there.

But further, Mr. President, I am not desirous of adding to the number of these States, whether the addition be free or of slaveholding States. I look upon it as a great calamity that the country should be placed in a situation which makes it necessary that other States shall be admitted into the Union. I think the value of a place in this Union is in inverse ratio of the number of States that compose it: the smaller the number the greater the honor, the power, the influence, the relative strength in the Union of the different members that compose it."

Aug. 6.   David L. Yulee.
Speech of Hon. D. L. Yulee, of Florida, on the Admission of California. Delivered in the Senate of the United States, Tuesday, August 6, 1850. W a s h i n g t o n: Printed at the Congressional Globe Office. 1850.
   23 pp.

The speech was a last ditch stand against the admission of California, with her proffered boundaries. Yulee spoke in support of his own plan submitted to the Senate as a substitution for the admission bill. It proposed to split California with an extension of the Missouri compromise line on the 36° 30' north latitude, establish a territorial government south of that line, and recognize the newly organized state government as a provisional government in the north until it is voted upon by her people as to whether she shall be a territory or a state. He said the organization of a state government was premature. According to the California delegation, on the first of August, 1849, the population comprised 13,000 native Californians, 12,556 foreigners, and 17,994 Americans, but of the American and foreign immigrants, less than three percent were females. "This indicates immaturity of social organization, and leaves us without assurance of the permanency of the population... In the next place, the constitution did not receive the votes of a majority of the persons in the country at the time of its submission... A third reason I will assign why Congress should refuse to sanction the proceedings upon which the present application is made for admission... The expenses of the convention were defrayed by General Riley, with moneys belonging to the United States, not appropriated by Congress to the purpose . . . They [Americans] comprise, I dare say, a greater amount of character, talent, energy, and enterprise, that was ever before thrown together in the settlement of a new country. But very few of them are yet owners of real estate, because the government, which is the great land proprietor there, has not brought it into the market . . .

and how is the state government to be supported?"

Aug. 10.   Hugh A. Haralson.

The Territorial Question. Speech of Hon. H. A. Haralson, of Georgia, in the House of Representatives, Saturday, August 10, 1850.

Printed in the Congressional Globe, no separate seen.

There was little in this speech upon the California question. Haralson accuses President Taylor of interfering in California, and through his promotion of a free state government, lost to the South about one-third of the territory acquired from Mexico.

Aug. 12.   John M. Berrien.

(Speech of Berrien, of Georgia, in the Senate.)

Printed in the Congressional Globe as part of a debate, with no caption, no separate seen.

Berrien felt obliged to give his and his constituents' views upon the admission of California. He objected to the irregularities in the formation of the State. "You cannot, in the records of this Government, find an instance in which a State has been created out of the public domain of the United States, by the action of an unorganized body of people, and then, without further action, admitted by Congress into this Union."

The second objection was a confused argument. "If California be a Territory; if an unorganized body of the people of that Territory be incompetent to form a constitution without the previous assent of Congress; if that assent is to be given to an act which, upon this principle, is in itself a mere nullity, then sir, the State which is to be admitted into the Union by this act is a State which is to be created by this act. I have some difficulty in demonstrating a proposition which appears to be so undeniably clear as this."

We agree with you, Mr. Berrien.

Aug. 12.   Lewis Cass.

Admission of California. Remarks of Mr. Cass, of Michigan,

in reply to the reference to his opinions on the Sovereign Power of Congress over the Territories by Mr. Berrien, of Georgia. Delivered in the Senate of the United States, August 12, 1850. (Towers, printer.)
    8 pp. Caption title.

Cass was one of a minority, now virtually extinct, who could upon occasion, with clarity and conciseness, reflect the true and original intentions of the Constitution. "I am the only man in the Senate, and almost the only citizen out of it, who does not believe, that this Government has full and unlimited power over these territories; though I trust there are many, both here and elsewhere, who have not so far forgotten the faith of their fathers, as to acquiesce in such a monstrous assumption of arbitrary power. Why, it is the very doctrine, and almost the very words, of the declaration act of George III, which our fathers resisted successfully — first in argument, and then in arms — that His Majesty in Parliament has the right by statute, to bind the colonies in all cases whatsoever . . . Whence do you derive such power? Put your finger upon a single clause or word of the Constitution, if you can, which gives it to you . . . Congress is vested with no attribute of sovereignty, as the foundation of legislative power, nor is the word itself to be found in the Constitution . . . Ours is a government of limited powers and of strict construction; and yet we so easily depart from its principles, that here is a strenuous effort to clothe this delegated legislature with sovereign power because sovereignty is an essential condition of an independent people . . . The proposition that Congress has constitutional power to legislate for the Territories contains the real doctrine maintained by the Senator [Berrien], and in words not to be misunderstood."

According to Berrien, the people of California had no right to organize a state government, nor was there a precedent for their procedure. Cass answered that "never before did Congress utterly neglect its duty, and leave a new and remote acquisition without organization."

Aug. 12. George W. Jones.
The Finances, the Territories, etc. Speech of Hon. G. W.
Jones, of Tennessee, in the House of Representatives, Monday,
August 12, 1850.
Printed in the Congressional Globe, no separate seen.

Jones expressed his willingness to vote for the admission
of California, but first, the bill to establish a territorial government for Utah, because it is silent on the slavery question, the
same for New Mexico, and the settlement of the Texas boundary. He preferred that California be divided into two, but he
was of the opinion that both would eventually come into the
Union as free States, so "it will be better to have one than
two free States."

Sept. 7. Jacob Thompson.
Thompson was a Representative from Mississippi. His speech
is given neither title nor caption in the Congressional Globe,
but it has the dubious honor of being the last. It was the final
effort of the South to gain some little advantage in the long
struggle over the admission of California. He offered a substitute bill, which authorized the admission of California, and
to form a territorial government for South California, that
portion of the territory below 36° 30' latitude (just south of
Monterey).

"The adoption of a territorial government for South California is demanded by the people of that country. The whole
South asks for the division as an act of justice. Every consideration of sound policy demands the division. We are ready
to accept the territorial government for South California that
you have given to New Mexico. In this, it is said, you will
get two free States: this is not certain, but it is certain that if
California is ever divided by her own consent, both States
will be free. That she will be forced to a division before ten
years, is to me morally certain."

The passage of the bill was hopeless, which was admitted
in the opening of his speech.

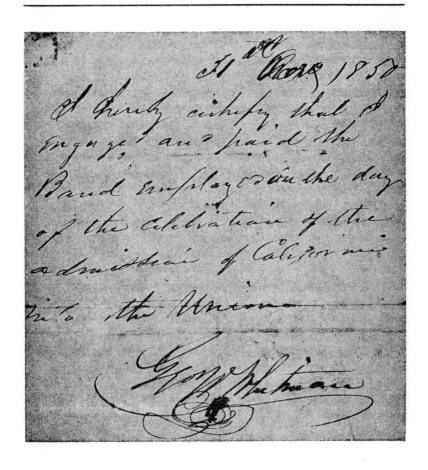

31st Oct. 1850

I hereby certify that I
engaged and paid the
band employed on the day
of the celebration of the
admission of California
into the Union.

Geo. W. Whitman